Forever Young

Forever Young

A Cultural History of Longevity

Lucian Boia

translated by Trista Selous

REAKTION BOOKS

Published by Reaktion Books Ltd
79 Farringdon Road, London EC1M 3JU, UK

www.reaktionbooks.co.uk

First published in English 2004

This is a revised and expanded edition of the book published as
Pour vivre deux cent ans © 1998 In Press Éditions, Paris

English-language translation © Reaktion Books 2004

This book is supported by the French Ministry for Foreign Affairs, as part of the Burgess programme headed for the French Embassy in London by
Liberté · Égalité · Fraternité
RÉPUBLIQUE FRANÇAISE the Institut Français du Royaume-Uni.

Printed and bound in Great Britain by
Cromwell Press, Trowbridge, Wiltshire

British Library Cataloguing in Publication Data

Boia, Lucian
    Forever young: a cultural history of longevity from antiquity to the present
    1. Longevity
    I. Title
    571.8'79

ISBN 1 86189 154 7

Contents

Introduction

Human beings are far from happy with their lot. Moreover we are alone – on this Earth at least – in asking existential questions. Intelligent enough to ask them we may be, but almost certainly not enough to find the answers. How can we come to terms with our brief lives, whose joys are too often mitigated by sorrow and which end, to all intents and purposes, in obliteration? Faced with this most unsatisfactory reality, three strategies are open to us.

First is the message of the traditional religions: nothing ends with death. One way or another life goes on, but in a different dimension. The 'double' of our material body – regarded as immortal – passes into the Hereafter or, possibly (according to the theory of metempsychosis), is reincarnated in a series of many different forms. Perhaps it is only 'afterwards' that true life begins.

The second strategy dissolves the individual into the community. Each of us is mortal, but humanity will live on. The only way to give meaning to our lives is to devote ourselves to some grand collective project. This way something of our ephemeral passage through this world will remain (*non omnis moriar* – 'I shall not die entirely' – to quote Horace). Ultimately what matters is not personal success but the realization of the potential of the human race (or of a particular community, people or nation). This way of seeing things is not so different from the religious attitude, except that it replaces the divinity with humanity in a form of 'secularized religion'. The modern period in particular has witnessed a proliferation of such religions, based on strong principles such as Nationhood, Democracy, Progress, Science or the 'Radiant Future'.

The third and last strategy seeks to go directly to the root of the problem by tackling human structural inadequacies. It aims radically to transform our condition, creating a truly 'new human being', quite different from the frail, ephemeral creature of today. Its most ambitious goal is immortality, or something approaching it – at any rate an appreciably longer and better life.

These three strategies have always coexisted; one or another, however, comes to the fore at different times and in different civilizations. For a long time the traditional religions seemed to provide the only useful answer, in the form of salvation. Then, in the eighteenth and nineteenth centuries, the West saw a gradual decline in religious belief and practice, with a parallel rise in the belief that human beings are capable of forging their own destiny. This resulted in the prominence of the purely 'social' projects of the secularized religions of ideology. Their aim was to achieve perfection and happiness in life and on this Earth, rather than after death.

Today this second formula too looks old and tired. The Western world has reached a level that, while certainly far from the perfection imagined by the apostles of Progress, nevertheless provides both functioning social and political mechanisms and an appreciable degree of well-being. As a result there are now fewer 'grand projects'. Might this be the end of history, as some have predicted? We are living ever more firmly in the present. The future, like the Hereafter before, is losing its appeal. Of course these two types of belief, the one focusing on Heaven, the other on the values of community, have persisted and will continue to do so; the numbers of people who run their day-to-day lives according to such beliefs, however, continue to dwindle.

Human beings must always believe in something. Never content with simply living our lives and looking no further, we aspire to the Absolute. The withering of the first two scenarios has left the way wide open to the third: the transformation of life. Although this desire originated in the distant past, it has found particularly favourable ground in the material and mental context of our time. We are becoming increasingly individualistic; we are used to leading comfortable lives; we expect to reap the benefits of our own lives and we do not want to die; we do not want to grow old. Perhaps this is asking too much. Yet today our search for a 'new life' has a major factor in its favour: science in general, and genetics in particular, already seems capable of providing effective methods for the biological 'redevelopment' of the human species. A new religion is forming: the hunt is on for eternal youth.

The chances that this project will succeed are hard to assess. The future is an unknown country and things will almost certainly turn out differently from all our predictions. On the other hand we can learn a great deal from exploring the past. The quest for long life has a history, and that history has two sides. One is real history: from Antiquity to the present day (with remarkable progress in recent years), human beings have managed to appropriate a little piece of eternity; we are living longer than our ancestors and we remain youthful for longer. The other is mythical history, whose ambitions go way beyond a few extra years. Without altogether forgetting real history, to which I shall return every now and then, it is the mythical history that I propose to relate. Of course we will be dealing here with fiction, with things many regard as not true. However the question of their truth remains open. Why should things that happen in our heads be any less true than those that occur in the material world? Human beings live on two planes at once, the world of reality and that of the imagination. While the two are distinct, there is continual traffic between them. Some elements of the imagination, such as dreams, utopias and idealistic projects, prove extraordinarily powerful. Some of them have stayed with humanity down the centuries and indeed millennia. It is only natural that human beings should try to make them real. Sometimes they succeed, sometimes not. It is this constant struggle between materiality and dreams that gives rise to history.

Perhaps, to return to our theme of longevity, we may find that today's scientific projects are not so different from yesterday's mythological fictions.[1]

1 Original Perfection

Antiquity

THE METHUSELAH MODEL

According to Judaeo-Christian tradition the greatest age ever reached by any mortal is 969; the name Methuselah has become a symbol of longevity. In recent years the absolute record for our time was set by Jeanne Calment's death at the age of 122. It seems we are far from our original perfection.

In fact even the vital energies of Methuselah and the other patriarchs were merely tiny sparks of the divine flame. Adam and Eve had been created in the image of God and were promised eternal life. With their expulsion from the earthly paradise human beings entered the empire of Death; however, biological decline was a gradual process. Adam lived for 930 years, his son Seth for 912 and his grandson Enos for 905. They were followed down the generations by Cainan, who died at the age of 910, Mahalaleel, who died at 895, Jared, who died at 962, and Enoch, who was borne up to heaven at the age of 365 without actually dying. Enoch's son was Methuselah, who in turn was father to Lamech, who lived to be 777. Noah, Methuselah's grandson, was 600 at the time of the Flood and went on to live another 350 years, making 950 altogether.[1] We do not know much about the life of Methuselah. His symbolic role is to provide a kind of link between the two founding moments of human history: the Creation and the Flood. He spent his youth with the elderly Adam (the first man died when Methuselah was 243), who may perhaps have passed on his memories of Paradise.

He lived until the year of the Flood, year 1656 of Creation, and the circumstances surrounding his end remain unknown. Did he die a few weeks before the cataclysm? He is certainly not mentioned as one of the passengers on the Ark and it is unthinkable that he might have drowned with the rest of humanity. A different method of calculation even suggests that he lived for a few years after the Flood, perhaps taken up by God, like his father Enoch before him, and set down again in some isolated spot after the waters had receded.

It would be useful to know more about this patriarchal society in which seven or eight generations lived side by side, a possible model for the humanity of tomorrow. Unfortunately, the Bible does not provide many details. These people were undeniably of a particular kind; they amassed years without growing old, apparently enjoying a very different distribution of the ages of life from that we know today. According to our bio-rhythms, a life expectancy of 900 years would have meant that childhood was prolonged until at least the age of 150; yet this was not the case. Some patriarchs became fathers at 65, and indeed 35; others, by contrast, did so much later. Noah's three sons were born when he was 500. Childhood and old age occupied much smaller segments of an entire lifetime: theirs was a world of vigorous adults. Something that the Bible also vaguely suggests, and which some exegetes have sought to highlight, is the physical aspect of our ancestors. They were probably taller than us; theirs was a world of giants. So the human race has been subjected to a two-fold involution, with both life expectancy and physical size shrinking at the same rate.

After the Flood biological decline became more accentuated. Noah's sons lived between 400 and 500 years, noticeably less than their father. After a few more generations had been and gone, Abraham, who was also one of God's chosen, lived no longer than 165 years, while Moses died at 120 a few centuries later. Lastly, with King David, we reach 'normal' history; David spent his last days in a state of advanced age at only 70. Human beings had become 'humanized', gradually using up their reserves of the divine elixir of life.

To a rationalist mind, the lives of the patriarchs were prolonged well beyond the limits of the possible. The figures given in the Bible, however, are really very modest compared with similar traditions from other peoples. The Indians attributed no less than 80,000 years to the first generation of human beings, and 40,000 to the second. In Mesopotamia ten kings together account for a period of 432,000 years; the last of these rulers, just before the Flood, ruled for 64,800 years. Reigns of 18,000 years are also recorded in China.

In this context, far from making exaggerated claims, the Bible is striking for its moderation and the air of authenticity lent by its restrained style and precise chronological account of the succeeding of generations. No one can believe that people might have lived for tens of thousands of years, but a few hundred? Why not? This explains why the Bible remained an authority to be referred to on longevity, as on so many other essential questions linked to human destiny. It is moreover not unique; it is easy to identify within it certain traces of the Mesopotamian legends, of which *The Epic of Gilgamesh* offers the best literary illustration, including a Flood. Gilgamesh, King of Uruk, reigned for 126 years; his ancestors were said to have ruled for 1,200 years, 420 years and 325 years, reflecting a chronological scale not dissimilar to that of the Bible.

The earliest conceptions of history were fundamentally pessimistic. In the beginning was perfection, in a world where the divine breath had not yet dissipated into thin air and human beings and gods were still close. This young, exuberant world was reflected in a young, vigorous humanity, the 'golden race' depicted by Hesiod in his poem *Works and Days*. Hesiod describes the members of this race living like gods, with nothing to worry them or cause them sorrow. They knew nothing of old age, for these were the days of perpetual youth. When death came, they simply fell into a kind of sleep.

At some point the Greeks realized that they had, after all, made some progress in relation to primitive times. Indeed it would have been difficult to regard the century of Pericles as inferior to the archaic period in Greece, and so a vague idea of 'Progress' was born (still a long way from the true religion of Progress that has so profoundly marked modern times). This notion of Progress was grounded in the past, ignoring the Future (a very vague concept indeed for the Ancients and matter for worry rather than hope). What the Ancients lacked was a Project. Where were they going? Nowhere, it seemed. Moreover the (relative) rationalism and optimism of the classical age did not last long. The late centuries of antiquity reveal a rising pessimism, a kind of intellectual and moral disorientation. Such lack of direction and confidence largely explains the collapse of the Ancient world.[2] This was the ground on which Christianity appeared and flourished, converting disenchantment into hope. For Christians the collapse of the Ancient world opened the way to the establishment of a new world, whether on Earth or in Heaven.

The world's exhaustion lies at the heart of the discussion by the Roman poet and philosopher Lucretius (c. 98–55 BC) in his poem *De rerum natura*. According to him the Earth had lost its strength and could only just manage to create small animals where, in the beginning, it had engendered gigantic beasts; fruit and pastures had difficulty growing, despite all efforts to make them thrive. Everything, the philosopher concludes, is nearing the grave, gradually dying, exhausted by the long path of life.

Three centuries later St Cyprian (d 258), one of the Fathers of the Church, described the ageing and exhaustion of the Earth and that of the human race occurring in parallel. Human beings, who once lived 800 or 900 years, could now barely manage 100, sure proof that the end of time was near.

Against this background of a general decline in longevity, some individuals fared better than most of their contemporaries.

The typology of these people is most instructive. Some were sages – indeed saints – while others were kings. Some Chinese sovereigns were said to have reigned for more than 100 years. King Nestor, sage and hero of the Trojan war, was said by Homer to have lived three lifetimes, corresponding to three centuries. The historian Ephorus attributed a similar age of 300 to the kings of Arcadia. Arganthonios, king of Tartessus in Spain, is said to have lived, depending on the source, 120, 150 and even 300 years. These people belong to a historical period that had already been mythologized, when marvels were still possible, at least on the individual level.

All these cases of longevity are united by the principle of original perfection. Those who live very long lives – first whole human races, later just the chosen few – enjoy the benefits of a cosmic energy that other people lack, arising from a fusion of the sacred with the profane that characterized the earliest times and continues to manifest itself every now and then. It is only natural that the saints should have very long lives and that the monarch, as an intermediary between human beings and the gods, should display certain characteristically vital traits, including longevity.

TOWARDS THE WORLD'S EDGES

At the level of the imagination we can observe an interesting correspondence between space and time. These two notions sometimes appear interchangeable and it can happen that one turns into the other. While time travel may pose insurmountable problems (although ultimately nothing is impossible for the imagination), there is still the other type of travel on earth, sea or through the cosmos. On each stage of the journey we explore landscapes and cultures suggesting the stages of our own past or future. The evolutionism of recent centuries has often drawn on indirect proof of this kind, rediscovering, for example, the distant past among the 'savages', in the 'primitive societies' that exist alongside our developed civilization, and the future, perhaps, among the extraterrestrials (in the nineteenth century Mars and Venus, the two planets closest to us, respectively represented the Earth's future and its more or less distant past).

The future dimension was of little interest to the Ancients; on the other hand they were very interested in origins. And where were these to be found if not at the world's end – converting time into space – on the boundaries of human habitation? The Greeks adopted and perfected a geographical schema that had originated in the Middle East. The inhabited world, the *oikoumene*, appeared as a great island surrounded by the river Ocean, beyond the far bank of which lay an indefinite, or at least unknown, space. The lands at the world's end, situated along the inner bank or on islands, displayed an enormous range of marvels and anomalies, as described by Homer, Hesiod and other poets of the archaic period. Their landscape was luxuriant, one of its essential elements being soft, flower-filled grassland. Here was where the gods and goddesses lived, such as Calypso on her island. Here also lived monsters, the Gorgons, griffins, Cyclopses and sirens, as well as those happy peoples for whom history ended in the golden age and who therefore knew nothing of our cares and miseries. The Ethiopians belonged to this ahistorical race: according to Homer they lived in joy and shared their feasts with the gods (just like the human beings of Hesiod's 'golden race'). They were part of the original amalgam in which the three

Lucas Cranach
the Elder,
The Golden Age,
1530, oil on
canvas.

components of the universe, nature, human beings and gods, had
not yet become separate.

Then, starting in the sixth century BC, the philosophers took over
responsibility for the world. They modified certain details, but the
edifice as a whole remained standing on its ancient foundations.
The river Ocean became a true ocean, with its adjacent seas. The
three continents of Europe, Asia and Africa took shape within the
great island. Nothing fundamental was changed; the relationship
between the centre (Greece) and the periphery (the edges of the
Ocean) were still subject to the same criteria and values. The greater
the distance, the more obvious the manifestations of otherness.[3]

According to Herodotus the Ethiopians are the greatest and
most handsome of all peoples; most live 150 years, some even
longer.[4]

An equally interesting case (again related by Herodotus), from
the other end of the world known to the Greeks, is that of the
Massagetes, a Scythian people living near the Caspian Sea. The
Massagetes know no limits where age is concerned. When one of
their number grows very old, that individual is sacrificed by the
others, along with animals, and the meat eaten at a family feast.
They do not practise agriculture but raise animals and are great

milk-drinkers. In addition, all the men live with all the women.[5] This corner of the world has remained apart from history and the norms of civilization. Longevity is simply one sign of their difference.

Nothing, however, can outdo India – as seen by the Greeks – when it comes to biological, social and moral strangeness. India is home to, among others, the Cynocephalae (mountain-dwelling men with dog's heads who, logically enough, express themselves by barking rather than speaking) and the Pygmies, who are extremely small. The Cynocephalae are notable for their long lives and may reach the age of 200. By contrast the Pygmies have short lives (eight years at most!), by analogy with their small size. The other Indians are no ordinary people either. Almost three metres tall and handsome, they never suffer any kind of sickness. Some live more than 100 years and some almost reach the 200-year limit.[6]

The prize for longevity went to the absolute geographical extremes: on the one hand were the Macrobi, a mysterious African people, on the other the no less mysterious Hyperboreans, who lived in the (undefined) 'far north'. Both were credited with a life expectancy of 1,000 years.[7]

The picture was completed by islands. The logic here was rather similar to that which governed the ends of the world, with the island seen as a world apart (our *oikoumene* being also an 'island'). The island worlds provided a space for the creation of an extraordinary diversity of landscapes, human beings and types of society (just as the Moderns would later make use of the planets, transferring the concept of the island from the earthly ocean to the cosmos).

A Greek called Iambulus landed on an island lost in the middle of the Indian Ocean and found himself in a kind of paradise, where the climate was always temperate. There was an abundance of everything in nature that is necessary to life. The inhabitants were handsome and almost two metres tall. Their curious abilities included speaking the language of birds and (since they had forked tongues) talking with two people at once. The men did not marry, but held the women in common, so the children were all brought up together. Theirs was a carefree life in some ways, but in others strictly regulated down to the smallest details of daily routines and food. It was basically a kind of communism. In these circumstances it is no surprise (since all anomalies go together) that they also lived very long lives, without suffering any kind of sickness and retaining the attributes of youth until the end. They willingly departed from life at the age of 150.[8]

Like the Greeks, the Chinese thought they were at the centre of the world, in other words in the only space of normality (indeed every individual and civilization is 'the centre of the world', judging others in the light of our or its own values). The space around China contained a great variety of strange creatures, with longevity ranking high among the imagined features of otherness. Some human species lived hundreds or thousands of years, and there were even Immortals living on islands untouched by time.

METHODS FOR ATTAINING IMMORTALITY

The location of 'long lives' at the end of time or the world was an expression of both nostalgia and the difficulty – not to say impossibility – of attaining great ages. The people who did so existed in a different dimension of time or space and the details of their physical appearance and way of life clearly revealed that they were not like us. The boldest of our own kind could always set off to the end of the world in search of immortality; indeed Gilgamesh did just that, only to return empty-handed.

Yet what good would mythical immortality and longevity be without the hope that they could one day be reached? Were they impossible dreams? Perhaps; yet perhaps they were also proof of a degree of feasibility: if such things have existed and still exist somewhere in the world, we can seek to penetrate the great secret and may also reach such levels of achievement – or at least a chosen few among us may do so. (Indeed it was precisely to justify this desire that almost limitless life expectancies were imaginarily located at the beginning of history and the ends of the world. Then what had been imagined turned into proof!)

So how was the goal to be attained? Here are some solutions.

The two great themes of approaches to longevity, rejuvenation and immortality, figured in many of the mythical narratives of Greece. Immortalization rituals might be practised on newborn babies, preferably involving an ordeal by fire to remove all principles of corruption. Something even better was found for Achilles, whose mother, Thetis, dipped him in the Styx. This made him invulnerable, except for the heel she held him by (a gap that led to his death during the Trojan war).[9]

Where rejuvenation was concerned, one recommended solution was the tree of youth, which, according to the historian Theopompus (fourth century BC), 'rejuvenates any who tastes its fruit'. There was also the indisputable expertise of Medea, the famous enchantress, who successfully rejuvenated Jason's father, Aeson, as recounted in detail by Ovid in his *Metamorphoses*. The feat involves a skilfully concocted potion (whose thousand ingredients include roots, seeds and flowers, a stag's liver and the entrails of a werewolf), followed by the first ever transfusion. Medea slits the old man's throat with a sword, lets the blood run out, then fills his veins with the liquid she has prepared. Aeson's beard and hair suddenly turn from white to black, his wrinkles disappear, his limbs regain their vigour and the old king becomes once more the man he had been 40 years earlier.

One method recommended by a great many immortality 'practitioners' was that of progressive spiritualization, involving a kind of dematerialization of the person. Asia was the leader in this field. Medieval sources attribute life expectancies of 200 and even as much as 350 years to yoga practitioners. Freed from the body's limitations, the mind imposes its will on matter. At the highest level man becomes superman and can aspire to immortality. A present-day example is offered by the immortal Babaji, a guru who lives in northern India. This holy man's body is immutable; he needs no food and eats only to please those who are eating with him; his fleshly shell casts no shadow; he leaves no footprints when he walks, and so on.

Chinese Daoism advises a similar strategy.[10] Its followers seek to tap and retain cosmic energy by means of particular methods of breathing, mental concentration and constant internalization, while also keeping their food intake to the minimum, so that they become detached from the surrounding world and its agents of corruption. Daoism's founder, Laozi, believed it was possible in this way to reach the age of 1,000; his successors raised the stakes. One Daoist text unhesitatingly refers to a life expectancy of 10,000 years for the most deserving.

At this point the boundary between life and death, ordinary life and the life hereafter, becomes vague. Once he had lived 1,000 earthly years Laozi planned to leave this world – without passing through death – and ascend to the heavens. This launched a veritable migration among the Immortals, some of whom gave every appearance of dying and were buried; when their tombs were later opened, however, they were found to be empty. They had a range of options available, from ascent to the heavenly Paradise, to setting up home in certain islands off the Chinese coast or moving to a high mountain near the country's Western borders.

Although still alive in the physical sense, they nevertheless lived far from human society, in the hereafter, the preserve of the dead. The immortal state thus remained ambiguous, neither life nor death, or perhaps both at once.

Vegetarianism must also be included in the range of practices intended to purify the being and combat the corruption of the flesh. It is quite understandable that the eating of plants should often have been linked to the prolongation of life. The many doctrines inspired by this principle, from antiquity to the present day, are more than simply dietary in nature; they advocate asceticism and a particular ethic. This was true of the religious current of Orphism in Greece and its philosophical expression, Pythagorism. The rejection of animal matter, the consumption of which could be associated only with death, and the eating of plants, as the source of life, were one element in practices aimed at spiritualization and the development of vital energies.

Nothing, however, is simpler or more effective than water. Its powers of purification and regeneration, which are moreover quite real in a more prosaic sense, are confirmed by a multitude of traditions. According to Herodotus they provide one explanation for the longevity of the Ethiopians, who habitually bathed in a spring whose extremely delicate water apparently had miraculous properties.[11] Rejuvenating springs are also to be found in many Indian and Chinese traditions. The Bible reinforced the symbol with its spring in the middle of the Garden of Eden, the waters of which later divide to form four great rivers. This universal belief also has its Christian version as the 'fountain of youth', a kind of 'annexe' to the spring of Paradise.

Clearly longevity is merely a stage or strategy here, allowing human beings to gain time by delaying as far as possible the irreversible moment of death. Ultimately the desperate quest is for immortality, and in a form not merely spiritual but also corporeal. Yet how can this body, which is so manifestly destined for putrefaction, be rendered immortal? The only conceivable way is to mark it profoundly with the spirit, to purify and transfigure it in the image of our immaterial double. Immortality is attained, if not necessarily through death, at least through the invention of a different body.

Sex also features on the list of methods to attain longevity, or at least as a symptom of success. It may seem a paradoxical companion to asceticism, yet such an association is not without logic: sex, like the spirit, is one of the essential manifestations of vital energy. Christian culture has completely broken the link between the two; it has long taught that sainthood cannot be attained through sex. Yet, originally, strength of spirit and vigour of matter were both part of the great primordial Unity. The Olympian gods knew all about this. Even more recent behaviour proves that mystical fervour and sexuality are not complete strangers; they can become fused in certain rituals, for example in primitive cultures and some modern sects. There is a 'Rasputin effect', an uncomfortable mix of sainthood and sexuality. That monarchs have often been credited with remarkable sexual capacities is not unrelated to their transcendent function.

Like longevity, frenzied sexuality is a sign of an exceptional nature, so it is hardly surprising that we so often find them together. A Chinese man who died in 1933 aged 253 is said to have 'worn out' no fewer than 24 wives in the course of his life; he certainly had time enough. We shall have the opportunity to meet a great many such people who are 'not really old', endowed with uncommon generative energy. Indeed what could more powerfully express a vitality that can withstand anything, allowing individuals to perpetuate themselves beyond the ordinary bounds of existence?

Even the holy were not always averse to such methods. As an aid to longevity the Daoist philosophers and holy men strongly recommended coitus reservatus, where the man restrains his own orgasm while ensuring his partner has hers. The semen thus retained was regarded as a contribution to the accumulation of vital energy, a constant preoccupation of all good Daoists. The best effects were to be obtained through contact at least ten times daily, with different partners aged preferably between fourteen and nineteen. Conversely it was not considered at all advisable to waste one's substance for the benefit of a woman, longevity being, of course, a matter for men. Mutual love between Daoists was a better solution; that way nothing was lost.

The most inoffensive of the sexual games associated with longevity remains that of the biblical King David who, in his old age, enjoyed the services of a young girl whose task was to warm his body. This can be seen as an example of the transference of vital energy from one body to another. It was an idea taken up by some modern theoreticians and, if rumours are to be believed, applied by certain elderly political leaders following the example of their illustrious predecessor.

PLATO'S JOKE

Should we take Plato seriously? The great Greek philosopher employed a particular method, using fictions to illustrate his theories without prior warning. He was the most fertile and clever creator of myths there has ever been. Some, however, took him literally. People are still searching for traces of an Atlantis that will never be found, and with good reason: the famous lost continent is nothing more or less than one of Plato's fictions, a story with all the appearance of truth, but pure invention from beginning to end. *The Republic* is another case in point: beneath the appearance of a political study proposing real solutions, Plato in fact wrote the first utopia, thereby inventing a genre that was to have a brilliant career.

His method of 'rejuvenation' was no less bizarre; to apply it required nothing more complex than the modification of the order of the cosmos. In his *Politics* Plato imagined a world in which rejuvenation would have become the rule rather than the exception. He started from the hypothesis that the universe moved in alternate, opposing directions. At the point where it changed from one to the other, there would automatically be a change in the course of life. The old would grow younger every day, regressing to childhood and ultimately disappearing into nature.

Having disposed of earlier generations in this way, life would be organized on new bases. Instead of being born of sexual union, growing old and dying, human beings would be born directly from the earth as adults and would then grow younger, ultimately dissolving into the earth, from which new lives would spring up. This provided no gains in longevity; lives would last no longer than our own, but would move in the opposite direction in a more relaxed and carefree atmosphere, since no one would be afraid of growing old.

This is no more than a page of Plato's philosophy; yet already it gives us a foretaste of science fiction.

ANCIENT MEDICINE: *pragmatism and mythology*

Let us briefly return from imagination to reality. The Ancients, particularly in Greece, bequeathed to us both their mythology and their science.[12] Although there was a continual exchange between the two (which continues today, since this is by no means the preserve of antiquity), this did not stop the Greeks, in the classical age at least, from drawing a distinction between the mythical level and the more prosaic level of concrete existence. Immortality and rejuvenation had their place in the domain reserved for mythology. On the 'ground' the reality was something else altogether.

It is hard to calculate the life expectancy of the Ancients in any irrefutable way. Anthropological analyses of skeletons, funerary inscriptions and literary texts provide the main sources for such a study; however, interpretations differ widely. One researcher records a life expectancy of 45 for men and 36 for women in the Greece of the fifth century BC, while another brings the limit down to 25 for the Roman empire of the second century AD.[13] However, one thing is certain: life expectancy was very low compared to that of today. This was mainly due to the very high rate of infant mortality, but the 'very old' were also rare. In practice very few people lived beyond 60 (although maximum life-spans of up to 100 years seem similar to those recorded today, the numbers involved are infinitesimal). Another particularity was the high rate of female mortality (due mainly to repeated pregnancies and their attendant complications). In our own period women live noticeably longer than men (at least in the developed countries); in antiquity this situation was reversed.

The doctors were not concerned with repeating the feats of Medea. Neither Hippocrates (c. 460–c. 337 BC), regarded as the founder of medical science, nor his emulator Galen (c. AD 130–c. 200) were great enthusiasts for the longevity of myth. Their main concern was to maintain health and cure sickness, possibly to improve and prolong old age, but not to reshape the human condition.

For two millennia the legacy of Hippocrates and of the Hippocratic school in general (for it is sometimes hard to distinguish the master's works from those of his disciples) encompassed the entire spectrum of medical research and speculation; longevity did not escape its attentions, whatever the original intentions of the father of medicine.

Let us now consider the three main elements of Hippocratic science, which we shall encounter again at several points in the course of our investigations.

First is the influence of geographical surroundings, and notably climate, which was highlighted by the great doctor in his treatise

On Airs, Waters and Places. People are different because they live in different surroundings, an argument that has come down through the centuries to our own period. It also has a bearing on longevity: some countries are more favourable in this regard than others. To give only two examples: in places subject to cold north winds men are more robust, and 'naturally they live longer there than elsewhere'; by contrast, for those living close to still waters 'longevity is impossible' and 'old age comes before its time'.

Second is the special emphasis on nourishment and insistence on the need for a harmonious lifestyle, providing a good balance between nourishment and physical exercise (the latter intended to use up the excess provided by food). 'Those who eat weak foods', explains Hippocrates, 'do not live long'. No food, however, is wholly good or bad in itself; it must correspond to the disposition of each human type. The biological career of individuals is regarded as depending largely on what they eat. This idea was to prove extremely durable, although there has never been complete agreement on the correct selection of foods to be recommended or avoided.

Last, but not least, the cornerstone of the medical philosophy of Hippocrates and his successors is the doctrine of the humours. This is based on the major role played by the liquids of the organism, for which 'humours' is the generic term. Everything depends on the balance between the four humours, blood, lymph, bile and black bile (Latin *atra bilis*, also known as melancholy). The last of these offers a curious example of biological and medical imagination; no one has ever found the slightest trace of this liquid (for the good reason that it does not exist), but that did not prevent numerous generations of doctors from swearing by it, on the grounds that Hippocrates wrote about it. Health and sickness were strictly dependent on the mix and interaction between the humours. This theory persisted in medicine well into the modern period.

The dynamics of the humours also explained ageing. Each age

of life was dominated by one of the four humours: youth by blood, adulthood by bile and then by black bile and old age by lymph. Blood is hot, lymph is cold. Over the years the human organism gradually lost its innate heat and, tangentially, its water (a point that rather contradicted the logic of the system; according to the theory, the organism should have become more wet, but apparently the reverse occurred), so that the body gradually became cold and dry: this was old age.

The truth of this biological schema was borne out by the inhabitants of the British Isles. As far as was known they did not grow old until they were around 120. The mythological reason for such longevity is clear: these peoples, seen from the Greco-Roman centre of the world, lived on the edge of the Earth (like the Indians, but at the other end). However there was also a climatic and medical reason: since the rigours of the climate caused their bodies to contract and become more 'dense', they retained their inner warmth for longer. Paradoxically, yet efficaciously it seems, heat was protected by cold.[14]

The doctrine of the humours owes a great deal of its long-lasting success to the almost mathematical rigour and air of perfection bequeathed to the system by Galen. This philosopher and doctor devised a faultless mechanism into whose workings he integrated several groups of four elements. There were the four constitutive principles of the universe: fire, air, earth, water; the four fundamental physical qualities: hot, cold, dry, wet; the four humours mentioned above and, as a result, four temperaments: sanguine, phlegmatic, choleric and melancholic. These elements could all be combined in a great variety of ways. It was a fine construction, and a perfect system to boot. Indeed its degree of perfection was rather greater than that of its adaptation to the reality of things. Reality being far from perfect, any perfect system is a direct product of the imagination.

But while the theory is largely a fiction, the conclusions drawn from it by Hippocratic medicine in relation to longevity were ultimately fairly moderate and practical. Live in favourable surroundings, maintain a balance of the humours, eat reasonably and do physical exercise (to ensure good digestion), such is the path that leads to advanced age (also presaged by particular somatic signs, so that 'having a greater number of teeth is a sign of longevity'). Once again, the aim here is always 'normal' longevity, a simple consolidation of ordinary life expectancy. According to tradition Hippocrates set the example himself. He was initially said to have lived 85 years, but this was later revised upwards to 90, then 104, then 109.

A life of any greater length or a return to youth seem to have been beyond the powers of Hippocrates and remained the domain of Medea.

Through the two figures of Medea and Hippocrates Greece bequeathed a twofold legacy: on the one hand the search for a different kind of human nature, which would manifest itself in part through a mythical longevity; on the other the less ambitious, more realistic approach to the good management of the span of time granted to human beings as they are. Two thousand years later, this distinction is still with us.

DEATH ACCEPTED: *the example of Seneca*

'One is never so old that one does not honestly hope to live another day'.[15] Seneca's words seem to open the way to a boundless life expectancy advancing by one small step at a time, day by day, into eternity.

In fact Seneca (*c.* 4 BC–AD 65), Stoicism's definitive representative and the most famous of the Roman philosophers, had concerns more pressing than longevity. As a good Stoic he believed that the problem of long life had been badly posed. For the Stoics nothing was more important than wisdom; the sage was in complete harmony with nature and destiny, including the inevitable moment of death. Of course, all things being equal, it was preferable to live a long life than a short one. Unfortunately, Seneca observed, people are very interested in the quantitative aspect, the number of years, but much less and often not at all in the qualitative aspect of the question. They seem interested only in accumulating years, with never a thought for how they use their time.

Is life too short? Seneca answers this question in an essay precisely entitled *De brevitate vitae* ('On the shortness of life'). Aristotle deplored the injustice of nature, which had granted human beings far fewer years than it had given to some of the animals. The reverse would have been fairer, because humans have so much to do. These are not the words of a sage, replied Seneca; let us not complain about nature, it has treated us well. Life is long when we know how to use it. Unfortunately people waste their time. In practice they live only a tiny part of their lives. Why should we ask nature for more, when we are incapable of taking advantage of what it has already given us? As we shall all die one day, the duration of our lives is unimportant; at any rate, it counts for much less than their quality.

Seneca takes a dim view of almost all activities. The mortals most worthy of contempt are those who are interested only in wine and love; however, public functions and high honours do not lead to perfection, since there is nothing more illusory than glory. The most powerful men secretly dream of rest, of a retirement that would allow them to find themselves; such is said to have been the desire of Augustus, which he never fulfilled. The inner life alone can save us from the ravages of time; we must find eternity within ourselves. The recommended method is that of 'active idleness', remaining aloof from 'practical' activity and the bustle of daily life and living in the mind. Seneca proposes a kind of philosophical 'disincarnation'.

Above all people should remember to make a good exit. The number of our years is of little importance: what matters is not so much the moment of death as its manner. A life, like a play, is judged not by its length but by the actor's merit; nothing influences the overall impression so much as the final exit.[16]

It is amusing to note that the man who wrote these words was himself no hermit. Seneca led an active public life and was not above worldly things. He was Nero's tutor, intimate with the imperial family, and became first a senator and then (in AD 57) a consul. Furthermore he took great care over his own well-being, amassing a colossal fortune. In this, it might be said, he showed a remarkable ability to live two different lives, the 'outer' and the 'inner'.

Whatever the case, he certainly made a good exit. On Nero's orders he opened his veins and died stoically, in perfect harmony with the doctrine.

Seneca's message remains that of making life denser rather than longer. Yet Seneca was not an isolated case; in his own way, and in the spirit of his philosophical school, he expresses an attitude that was widely shared in Greco-Roman culture. That a Stoic should accept death stoically was only natural. However the competing philosophy, Epicureanism (founded by Epicurus around 300 BC), did not see things so very differently. Its 'spokesman', the poet Lucretius, devoted a memorable passage to the matter in his great philosophical poem. The Epicureans did not look down on the pleasures of life (indeed they were accused of enjoying them to excess); yet, explains Lucretius, a longer life would offer no new pleasures; all has already been played out. Moreover the time gained would be insignificant compared to the time spent being dead. The eternity of death is the same for everyone, however many years they may have spent on this earth.[17]

Another heavyweight participant in this debate was Cicero (106–43 BC), the famous politician, orator and philosopher (of the eclectic tendency). At the age of 62 he wrote a treatise on old age (*De senectute*), proposing to 'rehabilitate' it. He describes this period as the most spiritual age of a human life, the crowning point of a career rather than its decline.

Thus the goal of the philosophers was not to 'change the world' (as Marx would later ask of them in a very different mental context), but to make people accept it as it is.

It would be tempting to say that the dignified resignation of the Romans in the face of death was merely a way of making a virtue out of necessity. If we consider the imperial families, a few emperors (such as Augustus and Tiberius) lived beyond the age of 70, indeed almost to 80; most of their sons, grandsons and nephews, however, died extremely young, often posing complex problems of succession as, one by one, the heirs disappeared. Furthermore, no fewer than six of the first twelve emperors (first century AD) died a violent death (killed or forced to commit suicide). Political assassination was such a frequent occurrence as to be almost commonplace, while circus games in which much blood was shed provided some of the most popular entertainments. In such conditions death was an everyday companion.

PLINY THE ELDER: *a rationalist*

The most important elements of ancient knowledge on longevity, as on many other subjects relating to human beings and nature, were collected by Pliny the Elder in his monumental *Natural History*. The famous Roman naturalist, who was born in

AD 23 and killed when Vesuvius erupted in 79, was not satisfied with a simple overview; he also proposes an exercise in correct reasoning.[16]

He shows no indulgence towards the old kings who lived 150 or 300 years, still less to the records mentioned by the geographer Xenophon (not to be confused with the historian of the same name), who ventured to write that the king of a certain island (whose name and location remain vague) lived 600 years and, 'as this lie was not enough', that his son lived for 800. Such temporal inflation is to be explained by the ignorance that reigned in ancient times and also by the different structure of the calendar. Some ancient peoples counted summer and winter as a year each; others confined a year to each of the four seasons. The Egyptians counted in single lunar months, which reduced their year to one twelfth of the ordinary length.

Here then lies the key to the mystery and the method that should be used to cut mythical ages down to their proper sizes. A person aged 1,000 must simply have counted twelve years in place of one; such individuals can certainly claim to have reached a respectable age, but no more than about 80. This is a fine example of ancient rationalism, and indeed of rationalism in any period. The myths are true, but they speak a different language and must be translated.

Then, his critical duty fulfilled, Pliny accepts without raising an eyebrow all the information provided by the census carried out in AD 74 during Vespasian's reign. In one region of Italy a great many people were identified as being aged over 100, sometimes by many years. Four were 130, four were somewhere between 135 and 137, while three others had already gone beyond their 140th year. A few years earlier, in the reign of Claudius, a record of 150 had been established. The naturalist Pliny regarded these figures as irrefutable, since a census is a totally different thing from a mythical tradition.

Among the cases of longevity Pliny includes women in a list that sees matrons rubbing shoulders with actresses. Terentia, widow of Cicero, lived 103 years and Clodia, widow of Ofilius, 115, while two thespians, Lucceia and Galeria Copiola, were still treading the boards aged over 100.

Why does life expectancy vary so much from one individual to the next? Pliny does not know, but, returning to his rationalist exercise, refuses to credit the astrologers with any insight. Their claim to use the conjunction of the celestial bodies in order to establish the greatest possible length of a human life as 112 or 124 years seems to him to be quite without foundation. People may be born under the same star, yet their destinies may be quite different; the shape of a life is not given in advance.

It is still amusing to note that the figures advanced by the astrologers are very close to the limits of around 120 years recognized in our own time. They are certainly closer than some of the records that slipped through Pliny's rationalist net.

LUCIAN OF SAMOSATA: *encouraging longevity*

Lucian of Samosata (*c.* 125–*c.* 192) is the presumed author of the short work *Macrobii* ('Long-livers'), which is entirely devoted to longevity and very rich in all kinds of examples. Lucian was a prolific satirical author, a kind of Voltaire of Ancient Greece. The authorship of the text is uncertain yet, although the experts disagree on this, all agree that it bears the stamp of Lucian's cultural circle and, in general, his way of writing. Some have also noted that Lucian's contemporaries tended to feel off-colour, encouraging meditations on longevity ('Longevity was a topic of interest and encouragement in an age of hypochondria'.[19] However, it seems to me that in fact they might have felt rather more comfortable in the Empire's longest period of stability, a relatively calm and less bloody time, and that this may explain why they placed a higher value on life).

This short work is bursting with fabled cases of longevity, including that of Nestor, who saw three centuries come and go and, better still, Tiresias, the blind seer of Thebes, who is said to have prolonged his career across six lifetimes (600 years). We should also recall the entire nations that enjoyed the privilege of long life, starting with the Seres (a vague name given to the people of the Far East, particularly the Chinese), who lived up to 300 years. Some authors attribute such long lifespans to the climate, others to the earth or to food. Lucian notes that the Seres drink only water; perhaps this is the explanation.

Most of the examples, however, are of 'normal' lives prolonged as long as possible – in some cases a little over 100 years, most frequently between 80 and 100. So it was ordinary longevity that interested Lucian (or the author 'hiding' behind that name); his work is a kind of encouragement to long life. Earlier successes prove the project's feasibility, particularly those of prominent people such as kings and philosophers. And how is long life to be achieved? Simply by practising moderation. To those who asked him to what he owed his long, happy old age, the philosopher Gorgias (who died, tradition has it, at the age of 108) replied that he never took the pleasures of the table to excess. So be moderate in all things: eat in moderation, take moderate exercise, and you will live long in good health.

ST AUGUSTINE: *from the age of the first humans to the immortality of the chosen*

The triumph of Christianity in the Roman empire, which became complete in the fourth century AD, established biblical references as models of longevity. The kings and philosophers described by the Greco-Roman authors gave way to the patriarchs of the Jewish people. Longevity became an argument in the Christian historical schema; a reminiscence of Paradise lost, it also prefigured the eternal life reserved for the Just in the Kingdom of God.

The Bible is an absolutely crucial source where longevity is concerned. It offers a complete and precise picture of the evolution of life expectancy, from the first man to the period in which it settled down at its lowest level. Everything is there, generation by generation.

Of course, it was first necessary to believe. However, for its authority to become established, at least in the eyes of the elite, the Bible also had to conform to a certain type of rationalist thought, of the kind we noted in Pliny's work. Should the biblical Truths be taken literally, or should they be interpreted, or indeed read symbolically? This long, difficult debate began in antiquity and continues to this day.

The age of the patriarchs was one of the problems to be solved. It could have been played down by means of the 'division' method applied by Pliny; but that would have diminished its role as a demonstration of original perfection. The patriarchs lived longer than people do today because they were closer in time to the Creation. This is the import of the debate in which, indirectly across the centuries, St Augustine (AD 354–430) opposed Pliny the Elder.

De civitate Dei (*The City of God*), St Augustine's most important work and for centuries a crucial reference work for Western Christianity, offers a close analysis of the problem of longevity. We learn that the age of the first generations has not been interpreted unanimously. Some looked at the Bible through Pliny's eyes: 'Let us beware', wrote Augustine, 'listening to those who claim that the years were calculated differently at that time from those of today, and that they were so short that ten were needed for every one of ours. Thus, according to them, when Scripture states that a patriarch lived 900 years, this should be understood as 90.'[20] Such rationalists were to be found even among believers; far from seeking to undermine the authority of Scripture, their aim was to strengthen it by making what it said about the long lives of the first men seem more plausible.

Thus, dividing his age by ten, Adam would have been only 23 rather than 230 when he fathered Seth. However on this point Augustine notes a difference between the Hebrew text of the Bible and the Greek version of the Septuagint. The reference to the age of 230 belongs to the latter, whereas in the original Hebrew it was only 130. Thus Adam would have become father to Seth at thirteen, and in that case his older son would have been born when he was only eleven. Another biblical character, Cainan, provides an even clearer example. In the Hebrew text he had a child at the age of 70. 'How can one engender a child at the age of seven?', Augustine rightly asks in an impeccable demonstration *ad absurdam*.

Moreover, an attentive reading of the holy texts is enough to reveal that, even before the Flood, the years passed by at the same rate as they do for us. There is no other possible interpretation of such chronological details as, 'The waters of the flood spread over the earth, in the 600th year of Noah's life, in the second month and the 27th day of the month'.[21] 'The 27th day' means that the months were of the same length as the months we know; it is no less clear that the years in turn comprised the same number of months (otherwise the year would be reduced to 36 days and the months, if they existed, to three days).

Yes, our ancestors lived very long lives, of that there is no doubt; yet their life expectancy raises other questions. How did they go about maintaining celibacy or, more clearly, containing themselves sexually for 100 years or more? Augustine suggests two possible answers. The stages of life may have been differently distributed in those days; adolescence would have come to an end around the age of 100. However a second hypothesis seems more plausible. The Bible is not a civil register, it does not provide a complete list of births: 'Scripture does not mention the oldest, but only those required by the order of succession in order to get to Noah and from Noah to Abraham'.[22] This is the genealogy of a single line of descent. Furthermore, the patriarchs might well have become fathers at the age of twenty; nothing proves it, but nothing denies it either.

A last element in the debate concerns the presence of giants in the earliest days of history. This was a fairly widespread belief, mentioned in a biblical passage as well as by some classical authors, including Virgil and Pliny (cited by Augustine), who thought that bodies had got smaller over time. Augustine was not content with invoking the authority of holy writ and other sources but, a palaeontologist before his time, also used fossils to back up his argument. He had seen with his own eyes, 'On the river bank at Utica, a man's molar tooth, so extraordinary that . . . it could have made 100 of our teeth of today. It was, I imagine, the tooth of some giant, since if the men of that time were larger than us, the giants were infinitely larger.'[23]

Long ago the Earth was inhabited by giants and, while their race should not be confused with that of ordinary men, the latter must also have been larger than those of today. Biological excellence was manifested not only in size, but also in longevity. If the existence of giants is proven, the same proof also holds, indirectly, for life expectancy. All in all men before the Flood were more physically developed and longer-lived than their successors.

Man became mortal because of sin; this caused his immortal soul to become separate from his body, which is subject to corruption. At the moment even baptism cannot heal this separation of body and soul, which will only come to an end with the end of time, the resurrection of the dead and the Last Judgment. The revived body will be reunited with the soul for all eternity. The damned will suffer punishment in their very bodies, while the chosen will live in a 'spiritual body' (where the spirit will breathe new life into the flesh), restored to all the splendour of youth, 'corresponding to the perfect age of Christ' (in other words about 30).[24]

The Christian philosophy of history is quite simply focused on (bodily and spiritual) immortality. The only problem is that the initiatory journey is particularly long and littered with pitfalls. Immortality must be truly deserved.

THE ABSENT WOMAN

What surprises us today, in all these discussions of longevity, is the near-invisibility of women. Of the dozens of illustrious, long-lived people mentioned by Lucian, not one is a woman. Nor does the Bible mention women in this regard. The patriarchs are named, but their wives are forgotten. Eve gets no better treatment than the rest, although she was no ordinary woman. She is just as much our ancestor as Adam, yet she is never referred to after the departure from Paradise. Did she die before or after Adam? We don't know. Apparently it is of no importance. Much later, in the Renaissance, an Italian painter, Piero della Francesca (c. 1416–1492) did think of Eve when he represented the *Death of Adam* in a fresco in S. Francesco, Arezzo. Adam sits on the ground, supported by his wife, who must therefore have survived him. Pliny is the exception where women are concerned; as we have noted, he includes them in his discussion. He long remained the only source in relation to female longevity.

This 'discriminatory' treatment can be explained to some extent by the objective situation I have referred to above: in practice women generally lived shorter lives than men. Yet the main cause lies in the (essentially masculine) understanding of the feminine condition. Women, thought Aristotle, were 'incomplete beings', they were in a sense 'failed men'. The Bible explicitly establishes a hierarchy: Eve was created from one of Adam's ribs. To return to Aristotle, men are by nature intended to live longer because they are 'hotter', whereas women are characterized by 'coldness' (and thus a certain weakness).[25]

This prejudice proved robust. Until recent times longevity, in its mythical manifestations at least, was generally discussed in relation to men. To challenge eternity was a virile thing, an exploit for men only. Like many other historical indicators, writing on longevity reveals the secondary position accorded to women throughout history.

AN OVERVIEW OF ANTIQUITY: *Greeks, Chinese and Christians*

Antiquity systematized ideas on longevity and established their main themes. Since then this legacy has merely been redeveloped. We shall sum up its main elements here.

First is the highly tenacious belief that human beings were by nature intended for a longer life of better quality than that which they have today. The situation does not match the 'ideal model' of life because something is not working properly in the society we live in, or in ourselves.

Secondly, and countering feelings of powerlessness reinforced by nostalgia for a world forever lost, we can already see the beginnings of a voluntarist strategy aiming to restore human beings, whether collectively or individually, to their original condition of excellence. Antiquity saw the first skirmishes in a long combat against death in the name of life. Some of the methods devised (healthy eating, favourable natural surroundings, spiritual quest) have been retained down the centuries, adapting to the changing social, religious and scientific contexts.

As for defining the ultimate goal of a 'long life', it was in antiquity that the main 'ceilings' were established. The first was 100 years, the ideal, and sometimes actual length of an ordinary human life. Then, a little more ambitiously, the figure was set at 120, the age reached by Moses. Still higher was the 150-year life expectancy of the island dwellers visited by Iambulus. Then we reach 200, twice an ordinarily long life, and a ceiling reflecting a certain logic: perfectly healthy individuals living in a perfectly healthy environment should be able to prolong their lives to twice that of 'today's' humans, who are plagued by sickness and all kinds of other problems and live in less favourable surroundings. In antiquity the Indians fitted this bill. These four ceilings of 100, 120, 150 and 200 years became major goals of longevity, whether real or mythical.

Once the two-century limit is passed, the imagination takes flight and nothing can hold it back. Why not hundreds, thousands of years? The ultimate goal is of course immortality, which is better sought through the spirit (Daoism, Christianity) than ordinary biology.

We should also note the ideological sensitivity of longevity. Since all imaginary elements are also caught up in ideologies, no fiction is gratuitous, still less the great myths that set humanity dreaming. In this light longevity appears as a mark of excellence, favouring some communities over others, men over women, the chosen – kings, philosophers and saints – over ordinary mortals, believers over infidels, and so on. The quest for longevity presupposes the more or less complete reworking of social and moral values.

These general traits should however be grouped according to three distinct models. The Greeks and Romans of the classical period, the Chinese and the Christians did not all see things the same way.

While extreme longevity is richly illustrated in Greco-Roman mythology and in legends of all kinds, the fact remains that, in 'real life', the Greeks and Romans generally resisted its temptations. They had already learned to distinguish mythology from reality and, though they may have deplored the brevity of existence, were resigned to it. Many philosophers took the fear out of death and questioned the use of substantially prolonging life. Medicine worked to similar ends, healing the sick and alleviating the ills of old age, without attempting to challenge the limit of death. The light of the theme of longevity shows us a civilization that invented scientific procedure, but was little drawn by transformism and had no project for the future.

It was China that first provided the example of a real strategy against death. Daoism set in motion a complex of practices (diet, breathing, physical exercise, spiritual development, sexual techniques) whose aim was to defeat time and attain a life expectancy measured in centuries or millennia, or even immortality. This quest, however, assumed a detachment from the world and involved a particular combination of pragmatism and an approach that was more mythological than scientific; it was thus in accord with the spirit of a traditionalist civilization, closed in on itself and almost static.

By contrast the Christian quest for immortality was seen in terms of a vast historical schema, focused on a supreme goal and aiming to transfigure the human condition. In its way it was the first global application of the idea of progress (which the modern period adopted and secularized). The aim was to renew the world and human beings. Thus Europe experienced an infusion of idealism and dynamism that would profoundly mark both its own history and that of the world.

2 By the Grace of God

The Middle Ages

SAINTS AND KINGS

No other period in the history of the West shows such coherence as the Middle Ages. In its classic phase, around 1000, its social mechanism functioned through the interaction of three main categories: the warrior aristocracy, the clergy and the peasantry, while its cultural synthesis was structured around religious principles and values. There was an enormous operation to 'consecrate' the world, quite the opposite of the 'deconsecration' that would begin with the Enlightenment. Theology reigned supreme among the sciences; the intellectuals, most of them clerics, looked at the world from the privileged observation posts of the monasteries. They had absolutely no intention of doing away with the pre-Christian legacy, and took over a large proportion of ancient knowledge; they also accommodated all kinds of popular pagan traditions as best they could. Christian theology, Greco-Roman philosophy and science, and Celtic and Germanic folklore were the three fundamentally different, indeed sometimes divergent, sources of medieval culture. The intellectual achievement of the Middle Ages was precisely to harmonize these contradictory elements by means of a unifying principle. Everything was adapted and integrated into the Christian framework, in an image of the world in which nothing happened by chance. Everything had a precise meaning and the supreme authority was God.

The human mind is drawn to the miraculous. In the Middle Ages this fundamental penchant, which can be identified in every period and culture (including our own technological society), found extremely fertile ground. There were many springs to feed its impressive torrent of miracles: first, of course, the mystical interpretation of the universe and the human condition (which gave God and the Devil the freedom to act as they chose); second the West's isolation from other parts of the world, which stimulated ideas of the exotic; lastly, a great collection of mythological figures and narratives taken from the Ancients, from folklore and, a little later, from the boundless imagination of the Arabs (the 'dreamlike horizon of the Indian Ocean', as Jacques Le Goff puts it).[1]

The conditions provided by the Middle Ages for real manifestations of longevity were far from favourable. Moreover the eternal life promised by the Church of course obliged one to die. On this point the theological discourse seemed confirmed and reinforced by the actual situation. The grim reaper was always at work: there was a lot of dying in the Middle Ages. In a society living at the lower limits of subsistence, life expectancy was poor; the slightest disturbance (for example in the climate, through heavy rain or drought) would cause catastrophes, famines and epidemics.

Time was getting shorter: individual lives were fragile and brief and the same was true of the life of the world. Everything was rushing towards an end that seemed very near: the end of time and the Last Judgment. Our time on Earth was devalued and its brevity accepted as a fatal consequence of original sin.

While the chances of real longevity were minimal, mythical longevity was fundamentally adapted to the theological discourse. The soul was put in a commanding position. Following St Augustine, Thomas Aquinas, the great thirteenth-century theologian, explained (in *Summa theologica*) that Adam's body was in its nature perishable even before the advent of sin; it was his soul that, through divine grace, prevented the process of decomposition from taking place (which was no longer the case after sin appeared). Longevity was an affair of the spirit rather than the body.

Here is the legend of St Sylvester, who was pope from 314 to 335. Emperor Constantine contracted leprosy and, on the advice of the pagan priests of Rome, was to bathe in children's blood (the curative, indeed rejuvenating properties of young blood). At the last minute the emperor halted the massacre and, enlightened by a dream, commanded Sylvester to be brought before him. The pope succeeded in convincing Constantine of the excellence of a very different method of salvation in the form of baptism. At the moment he received the sacrament, the emperor's leprosy disappeared as if by magic. His spiritual purification was accompanied by the purification of his body. This event (in 326) had important consequences: the emperor's baptism led to the triumph of the Christian religion.

It seemed that God's grace could maintain health and prolong the lives of the 'elect' (until they embarked on eternal life). The category of people rewarded in this way underwent a radical transformation. The pagan kings and philosophers dear to the ancient longevity 'experts' were left aside, leaving, of course, the biblical patriarchs, who were joined by the new category of major Church figures such as hermits, bishops and saints. Long life appeared as a divine gift to the most virtuous, establishing a further argument in favour of the pre-eminence of the Church, which acquired the stamp of excellence in the persons of its servants.

The prototype of the holy old man was St Anthony, one of the great figures of the early years of Christianity and said to have lived 105 years, from 251 to 356. Anthony spent almost his entire life in solitude or surrounded by disciples in the Egyptian desert, where he founded several monasteries. The Church honours him as the founder of monasticism. He also became legendary for having resisted a long series of temptations by the Devil (the

Temptations of St Anthony are often represented in Western art, due both to the exemplary nature of the story and to the fact that the theme offers artists an opportunity to portray all kinds of chimera and seductions). In this case longevity simply confirms and reinforces the message of a prestigious career.

There are accounts, however, of even more impressive examples, their names and records differing according to the sources and traditions. Thus St Simon (a somewhat legendary figure), second bishop of Jerusalem and St James the Less's successor, was said to have been crucified in AD 107 aged 120, the age at which St Patrick (fifth century), apostle to the Irish, is also said to have died. David (sixth century), patron saint of Wales, was said to have lived for as long as 170 years, made even more uncertain since the dates of his birth and death are both unknown. However, the record for the British Isles, which were rich in centenarians, is held by St Kentigern, also known as St Mungo, revered in Scotland (the patron saint of Glasgow) and apostle to Cumbria, who died shortly after 600 at the supposed age of 185; his example was often invoked right down to the present day, as a proof of 'feasibility' (for those optimistic in relation to longevity he was the perfect model, living appreciably longer than the ordinarily long-lived, but by a difference that was nevertheless more 'realistic' than lives prolonged over several centuries or millennia). Unfortunately this record was revised downwards; today his age is given as 85 rather than 185. His was not, moreover, an absolute record. A man named Séverin, bishop of Tongeren (in today's Belgium), consecrated at the age of 297, is said to have lived for 375 years.[2]

The best solution for those seeking longevity was apparently the monastic life. The vast archipelago of the monasteries represented a space that was already different, a kind of relay station between the Earth and Heaven. To adopt the monk's habit was, as

Georges Minois says, to 'enter eternity'; it was the best way 'to escape old age, to prolong and perpetuate oneself'.[3]

Then there were the kings, particularly the mythical ancestors. According to historians of the time, Pharamond and Merovech, the legendary forebears of the Frankish kings, lived 300 and 146 years respectively. As for Charlemagne, the twelfth-century *Chanson de Roland* turns the young man at the Battle of Roncevaux (778) – for the future emperor was only 36 – into an old man 'with a hoary beard', albeit no ordinary old man.

En vérité, dit le païen, je suis tout émerveillé
A la vue de Charlemagne, qui est si vieux et chenu
Il a bien, je crois, deux cents ans et plus.

In truth, said the pagan, I am quite amazed
At the sight of Charlemagne, so old and hoary.
I believe his age is 200 and more.

Charlemagne is in the pink at over 200 years old. He imposes his authority, not by wisdom alone, but also with his physical strength. On the battlefield his arm is still young. Once again longevity and holiness go hand in hand. The king communes with God, who agrees to perform miracles to grant his prayer; the angel Gabriel acts as their intermediary. As a living legend to whom God Himself listens, Charlemagne could not fail to receive the apotheosis of long life.

More curious is the case of Attila, king of the Huns. Although for the West he was the 'Scourge of God', he became the mythical ancestor of the Hungarians, to whom we must turn to enter his name on the roll of longevity. It should be understood that, in the Middle Ages, the Huns were regarded as almost fantastical characters existing in a magical context and only just human (people from the ends of the Earth). At any rate, according to the ancient Hungarian chronicles, Attila lived to a very advanced age, with an appetite for women that well reflects a certain version of the archetype (royalty–virility–longevity).

According to tradition Attila was 124 – not that great an age among the Huns; his father was still alive and head of his tribe in Asia. Despite his age, Attila had lost nothing of the ardour of youth. His palace was filled with a great many women, whose numbers were constantly swelled by further marriages. However love was to prove fatal to the king. On the morning after his wedding to yet another young woman he was found dead by his new wife's side. At the age of 124 you have to be a bit careful.[4]

This group, whose members include St Simon and Attila, seems rather disparate. What they all have in common, however, in addition to the clear stamp of the supernatural, is the role they play in the founding religious or political myths of the universal Church, the 'national' churches, the Frankish kingdom, the kingdom of Hungary or the Western empire. As a sign of permanence and of a special relationship with the Creator, longevity lends added weight to an underlying excellence.

THE FOUNTAIN OF YOUTH: *from Alexander the Great to Mandeville*

The fountain of youth ranks high among Christianized symbols of longevity. It was known in antiquity but the Christian interpretation meant that its regenerative qualities could at last be explained. According to the Bible a river rose in Eden and split into four branches. There was probably a secret channel linking the fountain to the waters of Paradise.

The popularization of this legend owes much to the *Romance of Alexander*, one of the works most widely read across Europe in the

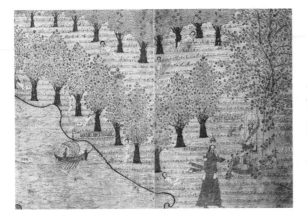

Alexander the Great on a paradisiacal island; the seated ruler of the isle has the Fountain of Youth at his feet. Illustration by Nastase Negrule for *Alexandria*, a Romanian version of the *Alexander Romance* (1790).

Middle Ages.[5] At the origin of the text lies the real adventures of Alexander the Great, the young Macedonian king who became emperor of the world (his empire covered almost all the world known to the Ancients). Although his was a true story, it seemed more similar to the exploits of the mythical heroes and was soon transfigured and enriched with magical elements. The *Romance of Alexander* gave the experts a hard time. The author is unknown (the attribution of the name 'Pseudo-Callisthenes' merely signifies a rejection of the fictitious authorship of Callisthenes, Alexander's official historian, who was ultimately killed on his master's orders) and there is uncertainty over when it was first written (dates oscillate between the Hellenistic period, second–first centuries BC, and the imperial Roman period, second–third centuries AD). In late antiquity and in the Middle Ages this text written in Greek, probably in Egypt, whose original is unknown, spawned countless Greek, Western and Eastern versions that, certain similarities aside, vary considerably from one to the next. The fact is that the fantastic tales of Alexander's conquests satisfied both its medieval readers' thirst for marvels (high prominence is given to the wonders of Asia and India) and their religious preoccupations, since Alexander's Asiatic journey seemed to take him ever closer to the earthly Paradise (located on maps of the period at the farthest point of the Far East).

The oldest known Greek version tells how the young conqueror approached the fountain of life, in a region where the sun never shone, in other words on the edges of the world; unfortunately it was his cook rather than Alexander himself who profited from its marvellous properties. The cook then offered a sip to one of Alexander's illegitimate daughters, whom he wanted to seduce. The king was jealous: he had conquered the world but stupidly missed out on immortality. He avenged himself by banishing the girl to the mountains, while the cook was thrown into the sea with a millstone round his neck. Of course both are still alive, the girl with the mountain demons and the cook with those of the sea.

This passage certainly does not have a very Christian air. However, in other variants the spring's paradisaical essence is described in more detail. Thus the French *Roman d'Alexandre* (a long verse composition of the twelfth century) explicitly states that the fountain's waters come from the river of Paradise. Those who bathe in it, even at a very advanced age, become 30 again (in other words the age of Christ and of the resuscitated bodies after the end of the world and the Last Judgment).

The Romanian adaptation (in turn derived from another Greek and Serbian variant) had an extraordinary cultural impact. Entitled *Alexandria*, it was the most widely read literary text in the Romanian lands from the sixteenth century to the eighteenth. One part describes Alexander arriving at an island where peaceful, happy men live in a natural paradise and, strikingly, go completely naked. The women are also conspicuous – but by their absence. They live separately, on a nearby island, surrounded by a fortress wall for safety and visit the men once a year. This arrangement enables the islanders to avoid the sin of sex, since they mate only to procreate. This was not the first appearance of such paired islands; they crop up from time to time in medieval sources, including the narratives of Marco Polo, who shamelessly claims to have visited them. The men's island is governed by an emperor, whom Alexander visits (as a colleague). He finds him no more clothed than his subjects, seated on a golden chair in the shade of a fruit-laden tree with, at his feet, a spring that is clearly the fountain of youth. The emperor makes Alexander a speech full of biblical references (he and his subjects are said to be descendants of Adam's son Seth), then offers him a flask containing the precious liquid, telling him to use it when he is old, so he can return to the age of 30 (although in fact it is well known that Alexander never grew old). The two islands of men and women are stages on the path leading to the earthly Paradise, of which they offer a foretaste.

Yet the cleverest denouement is that of a version circulating in Romanian folklore (which offers several completely reworked episodes of *The Romance of Alexander*). At the end of his expedition the emperor reaches the gates of Paradise, but is refused entry. However an old man or, in another version, a seraph, offers him some 'living water' (another common element in Romanian folklore, with the power to raise the dead and prolong life indefinitely). Alexander refuses (aware how great a burden eternity would be), but gives a drink to his horse, Ducipal, who is still alive today, perhaps waiting for another Alexander.

For several centuries the West remained closed in on itself, dreaming of distant horizons. Then came the moment when its inhabitants began to explore and conquer the world (the Crusaders were the first, followed by those who took the road to China and India, then the discoverers of America). On the way these travellers, traders and missionaries encountered many real places and peoples, which they then combined with the imaginary geography they carried in their cultural baggage. They placed more faith in what they thought they knew than in what they actually saw (indeed this happens on any journey: people see with their own eyes in accord with their own prejudices). One of the goals they sought was of course the earthly Paradise, located at the far eastern edge of the world. Columbus, who constantly translated real geography into an imaginary version (identifying America with the Far East and its inhabitants with 'Indians'), thought he was nearing Paradise at the mouth of the Orinoco (he regarded the presence of the equatorial forest and a great river that could only have its source in Paradise as proof enough).

It was inevitable that travellers on this route to Paradise would come upon the fountain of youth, which drew its waters from the paradisaical springs. One mortal who had the opportunity to taste the waters of this spring is Jean de Mandeville, or at least so he says. Mandeville was a very mysterious character: 'in principle' an Englishman (John Mandeville), in practice French, either way his status as a traveller is in doubt. He certainly never reached India or China, as he asserted he had. At the most he may have got as far as Jerusalem and the Middle East; unless he never even left his own garden. His *Voyages* (written in French around 1356) offer more of an 'image of the world' in the manner of the medieval cosmographies, and are rich in all kinds of invention. The fact remains that his book was immensely successful (250 identified manuscripts, a true medieval bestseller; few profane texts of the period ran to more than 100 copies).[6]

According to Mandeville the famous fountain was to be found in the region of India, at the foot of a mountain, a

fine, abundant spring smelling and tasting of all kinds of spices, and changing both scent and taste from one moment to the next. Whosoever drinks from this spring three times on an empty stomach is cured of his sickness, whatever it be. And those who live nearby and drink from it often never have any sickness and seem to be always young. I drank from it three or four times, and feel in better health as a result. Some call it the Fountain of Youth, because he who drinks from it always seems young and spends his life free of sickness. Such is its power that this spring is said to come from the earthly Paradise.

Mandeville confirmed Alexander, and Alexander supported Mandeville. Besides, what medieval reader would have doubted the account of a traveller who had seen with his own eyes and drunk with his own mouth?

THE OTHER WORLD: *the Irish model*

The most certain way to attain immortality is apparently to die, thereby being transported into a world where death does not exist. This was precisely the dilemma that the quest for immortality sought to resolve: how to gain immortality (or 'near-immortality') without passing through death. Yet death is not the same from one culture to the next. In the Greek Hades the dead, reduced to the state of 'shadows', continued a diminished, joyless existence – not a very exciting prospect. Meanwhile the Christian hereafter, full of hope for the deserving, was not without its disadvantages. It assumed an initial phase of painful and frustrating separation of body and spirit, the risk of eternal torment for sinners (and who has never sinned?) and, for the faultless, joys so virtuous they might be better left untasted.

Perhaps the Celts had found something better. Their beliefs, chiefly perpetuated through Irish folklore, aimed to render the hereafter closer and more human. Barriers were reduced to the minimum and crossing points increased in number. The *sid* – the Irish word for the other world and significantly also known as

Mag Mell (the plain of pleasures), *Tir Taimgire* (the promised land) and *Tir na nóg* (land of eternal youth) – was usually to be found in a land (an island) beyond the waters, to the west of Ireland; however, sometimes it is close by, in the hills or under lakes. It is a scattered world, not subject to the spatial imperatives of our own. Sometimes it is enough simply to cross a river or enter a cave to find oneself in its antechamber.[7]

At any rate, the atmosphere in these places leaves nothing to be desired. Everyone's wishes come true, particularly for those who appreciate women (truly magnificent here) and good food. The other world could not be described as a place for ascetics. The dominant note of sensuality (a never-ending party) was later attenuated – though it never completely disappeared – by Christianity, whose own project was to merge this relaxed Paradise with its own virtuous and hieratic version. The resulting modifications can already be observed in the voyage of St Brendan, an Irish monk of the sixth century. This is an entirely fictional text, written much later, around the tenth century, and recounting the Atlantic trip made by Brendan and his fellow monks. After a very long time at sea they reach the island of Paradise, but are not allowed to enter; from far away they hear the chorus of angels.

There is a continual to-ing and fro-ing between the other world and ours. Attractive women appear from time to time, inviting certain mortals (men of course) to follow them to the land of eternal youth. This is what happens to Oisín, one of Irish folklore's most prominent heroes. While out hunting he is contacted by Princess Niamh, a beautiful young woman who has come from the other world on her white horse. On reaching the 'Kingdom of Youth' they get married and have three children, two sons and a daughter. Time passes . . . or rather does not, since this is eternity.

Sea voyages were particularly likely to lead to the other world, or some of its outposts, the most attractive being the 'Island of Women', goal of the voyage of Bran. Bran was an Irish king who – also tempted by a woman from elsewhere – set off with 27 companions in search of the famous island. They managed to find it and spent some time there in good company. A similar trip was made by Mael Dúin and seventeen companions. After visiting no fewer than 33 islands, each with its own peculiarities, the men landed on the island of women, where they were received by the queen and her seventeen daughters. It is not hard to guess what happened next. The pleasures of bed and table follow one after the other in quick succession, perhaps with a certain monotony.

Imram (plural *imrama*, meaning 'rowing about') is the Irish word used to refer to this type of voyage to the other world. The close relationship thus established between the two planes of life attenuates the idea of death to the point of dissolving it away altogether. Death appears not as a break but rather as a continuation of life on a better plane of existence. Not only is the body not denigrated, it is invited to partake fully of food and love, the basic pleasures of life. These islands of the blessed are located at once in the other world and in our own; the boundary almost disappears, the interpretation remains open. Rather than a different life in a different world perhaps what is described here is more an extension of earthly life in a different part of the world, where time is no longer master: in which case death is simply replaced by travel.

Staying in a space designed according to a different logic, however, can pose a few problems to travellers. It is a perfect world, no doubt of that, but perhaps a little too perfect. The unexpected, that salt of life, is entirely missing; the same film plays on a loop into infinity. As a result there comes a time when our heroes start remembering the world they have left behind, with not just all its imperfections, but also its attractions. Nostalgia drives them to tear themselves away from their beguiling companions and set off on the journey home. Oisín, Bran and Mael Dúin and their companions all return to their native land.

Return is not without risk. Time has a different meaning in these parallel worlds. Hundreds of years may have passed for mortals in the meantime. Here is Oisín's homecoming:

> After three hundred years Oisín returns to Ireland on a white steed, with the warning from Niamh not to dismount, 'for if thou alightest thyself, thou wilt be an old man, withered and blind'. On his return Oisín found the famous fortress of the Fianna at Almu [Hill of Allen, Co. Kildare] overgrown and unguarded. Then, at Glenasmole ['glen of the thrushes'] in Co. Wicklow, a crowd of men asked his help in raising a huge stone onto a wagon. He stooped to do so, but the reins snapped and Oisín fell to earth. The white steed returned to the Otherworld, and Oisín became an old man.[8]

No culture can rival the richness and coherence of the Irish *imrama*; however a similar scenario is to be found in some narratives from different traditions. A text written in the thirteenth century in northern Italy (using and adapting an oral source) tells the story of a young lord guided by an old man – who is really an angel – on a voyage to an enchanting land that can obviously be assimilated to Paradise. He stays there for 300 years in a beatific state, unmarked by the passage of time, but then returns to find the old places unrecognizable. A monastery has been built where his castle once stood and his family are all dead. Now that he is back in the world where time kills, the young man quickly ages and is claimed by death.[9]

A Romanian tale tells a similar story, with the difference that this time the Christian element is absent, proof of the existence of an older or better preserved 'layer' of folklore. An emperor's son travels the world looking for a country where old age and death are unknown. He succeeds in reaching his goal, marries a fairy and enjoys many days of carefree happiness. Then suddenly he remembers his nearest and dearest and, giving way to an irresistible desire to see them again, goes home. Time begins to fly past once more and at every stage our hero grows older, eventually falling into the arms of death amid the ruins of his palace.[10]

THE TIME OF ROGER BACON

The period of the late Middle Ages (twelfth–thirteenth centuries) is rather out of tune with the preceding centuries, since it saw an opening towards the Renaissance and the early modern period. It was a period of demographic, technological and cultural growth, when Western society began to advance and expand, decisively marking the world's destiny right up to the present day. Theology still held the reins, but appreciable efforts were being made to combine it with investigations of a more scientific cast. Ancient Greek and Roman texts came back into circulation, while the influence of Arab science, more advanced than its European counterpart, was felt more strongly (this science was moreover highly dependent on the classical Greek sources on the one hand, and on particular procedures taken from alchemy, astrology and magic on the other; we should beware of trying to 'modernize' medieval scientific thought too greatly, be it Arab or European). Belief in revealed Truth was increasingly matched by an entirely human search for hidden truths by means of observation and experimentation. In relation to our subject of longevity, the Bible remained the fundamental source, but was already being supplemented by purely medical considerations taken from the works of Hippocrates, Galen and Avicenna (the Europeanized name of the great Arab doctor Ibn Sina, 980–1037, disciple of Hippocrates and Galen, whose *Canon of Medicine* dominated European medical practice and teaching for several centuries).

Alchemy had a prominent place among the West's new branches of knowledge. The Chinese Daoists were the first to practise this art. Alchemy was also known to the Indians and the Hellenistic world, mainly in Egypt (in late antiquity), from where it passed to the Arabs and then to the Europeans in the twelfth century, when they were discovering Arab science and philosophy (and indeed, through the Arabs, the forgotten ancient Greek sources). In the thirteenth century alchemy was already in vogue in the West and remained prominent until the sixteenth century.[11]

Alchemy is both a technique and a form of asceticism. For its adepts, the transmutation of elements (the quest for gold) was simply the material dimension of a far more subtle and ambitious project, whose aim was to transmute the human spirit and bring about the purification and transfiguration of human beings. Alchemical metallurgy, the strongest symbols of which were gold and mercury (the latter extracted from cinnabar, a red sulphur symbolically similar to blood), was a means of assisting this metamorphosis. The supreme goals of alchemical researches were the philosopher's stone and its liquefied manifestation, the elixir of life. These two would provide knowledge of the Absolute and the means to change the human condition.

Daoism expressly linked alchemy to the quest for longevity, and indeed immortality. The Arabs, being more measured, concentrated on its medical applications (the treatment of illness). But the West wanted more. The ambitions of the European alchemists were just as grand as those of their Chinese colleagues (of whose work they knew nothing). In the fourteenth century they developed the concept of the *Ars magna* (the 'Great work'), which would lead to the creation of a 'superman' with longevity to match. The alchemists hoped to rid themselves of corruptible flesh without passing through death, by transforming the human organism into a 'glorious body', like that of Adam before the Fall and those of the elect following the Last Judgment.

Without explicitly disassociating themselves from the Church, alchemists trod an independent, parallel path between science and theology.

This context of turmoil saw the appearance of an exceptional body of work, at once undeniably original and yet adapted to the spirit of the age, by the English Franciscan friar, Roger Bacon (c. 1220–after 1292), known as the 'admirable doctor'. A non-conformist, Bacon advocated an open science, founded on experimental method. His texts (the most important of which are collected in his *Opus majus*) manifest an approach that is at once both theological and scientific, in which the seeds of modernity can already be identified alongside a traditional strain of magic and alchemical speculation. Bacon believed in the human capacity to discover and appropriate the secrets of nature. He believed that human beings could perfect themselves using their own powers and means. His work confirms the individualistic, voluntarist aspect – the 'Faustian' element – in the Western attitude.

Bacon can be regarded as the father of the 'science of longevity', having made the first major individual contribution in the field.[12] As we have seen, there was no shortage of traditions, hypotheses and methods; Bacon, however, sought to impose a discipline on this body of knowledge, using an approach that respected biblical tradition, yet which he regarded as also pragmatic and experimental. His studies of longevity suggested a nostalgia for original, distant near-perfection, but also indicated a method that might restore the excellence of the earliest times. If religion proved that human beings had originally lived very long lives, science could re-create this original condition, or something very similar.

Man was designed as an immortal being, says Bacon in a chapter of his essay entitled *Epistola de secretis operibus naturae et artis* ('Letter concerning the Marvellous Power of Art and Nature'). He lost this condition after the Fall. Yet, even after the advent of sin, an ordinary human life then lasted almost a thousand years. This meant that the current reduced length was just an accident, the product of a deficient health regime and errors of a moral order. Man had eroded his biological capital through all kinds of imprudence. It was therefore perfectly legitimate to devise methods that might enable life expectancy to return closer to its natural limit of a thousand years (perhaps a little less, given that we have to contend with the great weight of heredity).

However, anyone hoping to find revolutionary arguments in Bacon's texts on longevity is destined for disappointment, since they are certainly not among his more innovatory contributions. For a rebel, he follows the 'authorities' rather too closely – but then a mythological challenge can only be met by mythological means. One cannot ask a thirteenth-century friar to solve a problem that still remains beyond the grasp of today's scientists.

Bacon dutifully adopts the theory of humours. Like his Greek and Arab teachers, he believes that, as the body ages, it loses heat and dampness. This is the process that must be delayed as effectively as possible. The remedy lies in a healthier regime, one certainly more respectful of the natural balance in the matter of food, rest, activity, passion and our relationship with the environment.

Bacon devoted an entire study to the 'treatment of old age' and the 'preservation of youth', in which he recommends a diet based on meat, egg yolks and red wine. He also includes certain more exotic recipes, including one inspired by Avicenna that involves boiling vipers in salt water and serving them with an accompaniment of red wine.

However, there is more to Bacon's methodology than this. The admirable doctor's ambition was to discover a universal remedy, the famous philosopher's stone or elixir of life that was also the goal of the alchemists. Bacon includes some formulae along these lines. Apparently, certain facts prove the solid basis of such research. Thus it was believed that 'stags, eagles and snakes become young once more through the powers of plants and stones', proof that nature had 'secrets', which were known and put to use by certain initiates. There is no other possible interpretation of the marvels experienced by a humble Sicilian peasant. This man was ploughing his fields when he came upon a gold vessel containing liquid. Believing the liquid to be dew, he washed his face in it and drank some. At once his body and mind were made new; he became good and wise and was appointed messenger to the king of Sicily.

No less edifying is the case of a German taken captive by the Saracens, who gave him an elixir that prolonged his life to more than 500 years. The Arabs are widely reputed as accomplished doctors and alchemists and certainly knew a thing or two. One of their master alchemists, known here by the Latinized name Artephius, penetrated the secrets of the animals, herbs and minerals and reached the fine old age of 1,025 (more than Methuselah – not an entirely orthodox argument for a friar).

Then there is the English lady who went looking for her white doe and found an ointment with which the gamekeeper covered his entire body, all except the soles of his feet. This gamekeeper lived for 300 years without illness, apart from pains in his feet (an 'infirmity' suggesting a reworked, less serious version of Achilles' heel). So it's true, such remedies do exist and there is nothing utopian in the project of increasing life expectancy, perhaps several-fold.

The list of occult remedies suggested by Bacon contains seven fundamental principles. The first lies buried in the earth and finds expression through gold; the second is found in the sea and materializes in pearls; the third slides over the earth as snakes, known for their capacity for rejuvenation by changing their skin. (There is nothing better for health and longevity than eating viper meat; even more effective, though, is the Ethiopian dragon, very hard to come by in Europe, but which explains the remarkable longevity of the Ethiopians.) The fourth principle grows in the air as rosemary, a shrub long appreciated for its curative and rejuvenating powers; the fifth acts through the vital energy of the noblest of animals or, more precisely, the heat or exhalation of healthy young people (preferably female – King David's method – although, according to Galen, even applying a small child or fat little dog to one's belly would do). The sixth principle is found in products taken from animals known for their longevity, in this case the stag (which, according to the ancient authors, lived a very long time), through the medical use of the bones found in its heart; the seventh and last is the aloe plant brought from India. There is nothing new in these remedies, which Bacon had come across in the course of his reading. However for him the 'scientific' aim was to combine them and establish doses that would ensure maximum efficacy.

It is tempting to state that this is not science (although science is never singular, but always plural, each period to its own). Of course we are a long way here from the 'experimental science' Bacon proclaimed. His 'experiments' on longevity were exclusively carried out in his head. His solutions are clearly pre-scientific when judged from the point of view of modern science. His intentions, however, are strikingly modern. With Roger Bacon longevity is integrated into a strategy for action. That which is possible and can be envisaged must be translated into fact. Religion shows the way, but it is up to man to act. The scientific adventure of modern times starts with this unusual friar.

3 The Body Strikes Back

The Renaissance

The Renaissance is a rather disorientating time, when the most diverse trends intersected. Generally seen as a prelude to modernity, as in some ways it is, it was at the same time an extension of the Middle Ages. In addition it was a kind of mirror of antiquity: its artists and scholars sought to get as close as possible to the ancient cultural model.

The Middle Ages had accorded greater importance to the Kingdom of God than to earthly existence. The modern period has reversed this trend, gradually distancing itself from the divinity. The Renaissance trod a middle path between these two opposing movements, attempting to forge a compromise between Heaven and Earth, human beings and Providence, free will and destiny. Its thirst for freedom and assertion of individuality and individualism led it away from the Middle Ages. The human body is one of its most characteristic symbols, a favourite theme of its artists. Their pictures clearly display the 'triumph of the flesh', in striking contrast to the hieratism of medieval art. In this context youth and longevity are given a value as great as that of the salvation of the soul; yet the soul's salvation continues to matter. Passionately humanist, the Renaissance was equally passionately religious – Heaven and Earth at the same time. Except that the increased dose of freedom and rise of individualism also overflowed into the religious domain. Medieval coherence gave way to diversity in the form of a proliferation of churches (with the Protestant Reform) and the growing independence of parallel researches such as astrology and alchemy, hitherto closely supervised by a Church concerned to maintain its authority. All the same, we are still a long way from modern rationalism; 'transcendent' approaches to longevity and immortality expanded and proliferated.

With the Renaissance the quest for longevity found one of its great teachers. His name was Lodovico Cornaro and he was born in 1467 to an illustrious Venetian family. In his youth he led a dissolute life, blatantly unsuited to his delicate constitution, and had ruined his health before he was 40. At this point, sensing that death had him in its sights, he took the heroic decision to change his ways completely and do the exact opposite of what he had done in the first part of his life.

Feasting gave way to a draconian diet: twelve ounces of solid food and fourteen of liquid (about 350 and 400 grams respectively) was the maximum the 'new' Cornaro allowed to pass his lips from morning till night – no more than survival rations. And the miracle happened. The prematurely aged man began to grow younger. He deviated only once – and then by very little – from his diet. Following the advice of friends who were intrigued by the strictness of his regimen, Cornaro added two ounces to his menu, making fourteen ounces of solids and sixteen of liquids. It almost made him ill and he at once returned, definitively this time, to his usual rations.

Comaro was a man given to excess who managed to take even abstemiousness to excess. The years passed and the patient grew better and better. At the age of 83 he assessed his own health as follows: 'I am in perfect health, I ride a horse unaided, I can climb not just a staircase but a hill without help from others; I am cheerful, good tempered, content, without perturbations of spirit or worries of any kind.'

The whole world had to know about this experiment. Cornaro began to write. In 1550 he wrote his first essay praising the merits of temperance, to be followed by three others on the same theme. All four were published in a volume entitled *Discorsi della vita sobria*, published in Padua in 1558. The author was already 91 years old; what better demonstration could there be of his method's validity. He ended his life aged nearly 100. This was no doubt a long way from some mythical records, but for a man who had almost died young, it was a fine victory over death.

Cornaro's attitude is marked by a goodly dose of realism. The aim is to consolidate what we have rather than to take flight for the upper regions of mythology. People should take care of their health and prolong their lives as much as possible, without nurturing the illusion that they can replicate the achievement of Methuselah. His approach does not seek to go beyond the limits of an ordinary life; its target is a long and vigorous old age, free of the usual ills.

However, this does not mean that Cornaro's project has no mystical dimension. He advocates an asceticism similar to that practised by monks and saints. In his own way he is the proponent of a kind of dematerialization. But though he looks to Heaven, he also looks to Earth. He is seeking the salvation of both his soul and his body; there is no contradiction between the two. Paradoxically it is asceticism that enables him to enjoy life more and makes life a better preparation for the journey into the hereafter:

Many people are amazed to see me live a double life, that is an earthly life in my deeds and a heavenly life in my thoughts.

The latter fills me with joy through the certainty that I have of enjoying it for all eternity, thanks to the goodness and mercy of God. I savour earthly life, the reward of my temperance, a life that is agreeable to God, full of virtue and free of vice.

Temperance is within everyone's reach and, once generally adopted, will change the face of the world. Human beings will come to resemble the fathers of the Church, who lived 120 years: 'like them they will perform miracles, will be healthy, satisfied and full of joy, while most are now sick, sad and bored'. 'How fine and pleasant the world would be with such a way of life!'

Despite Cornaro's efforts to achieve a harmonious combination of bodily longevity and immortality of the soul, his strategy places the greatest emphasis on valuing earthly life. The secularization and individualization of the quest for longevity are having an impact. Earthly life is starting to become as interesting as the life hereafter; already it can be seen as a good in itself. Cornaro is simply giving his own expression to his contemporaries' thirst for living.

Moreover he is not alone in thinking about improving old age and prolonging life. This period saw a proliferation of 'longevity guides', full of practical advice and addressed to all. Works of this kind (invented by the sixteenth century) reveal a particular interest in, and general 'democratization' of the fight against time.

DRASTIC MEASURES

Some preferred more drastic measures to Cornaro's own modest recommendations, and were aiming at an infinitely higher ceiling than the Venetian ascetic's lowly 100 years.

Alchemy was at its peak in the sixteenth century. There was never a better time to find a recipe for the elixir of life than the early modern period, still so hungry for miraculous solutions.

Freed from the theological hindrances of the Middle Ages, which had presented Roger Bacon with a long list of problems, alchemy's proponents unhesitatingly threw themselves into the search for the *Ars magna* and bodily immortality.

One fascinating case is that of Paracelsus (1493–1541). In a combination fairly typical of the Renaissance he was at once physician and alchemist, man of science and magician. Paracelsus was always on the look out for the secrets of life, hoping to restore human beings to their original biological perfection. He had very fixed ideas about longevity, ridiculing Cornaro's hard-won 100 years. His arguments are in fact very similar to those of Bacon. In his dissertation on the subject entitled *De vita longa*, he writes that a truly long life should last for 900 or 1,000 years – six centuries at the very least – a model clearly suggested by the Bible. The first men knew of hidden principles that were later forgotten, such as the properties of metals and minerals and magic formulae; these had enabled them to live almost millennial lives. All that was required to prolong life was the rediscovery of these principles. Paracelsus's quest was essentially pragmatic, drawing on, yet distanced from, the theological view of longevity. It was also infinitely better than Cornaro's method, being less demanding with better results.

The sixteenth century was also the century of astrology and the prince of astrologers, Nostradamus (1503–1566). When necessary astrology could also be used as an aid to longevity, as it taught how to match one's life to the movements of the stars. A seventeenth-century astrologer at the court of the Elector of Brandenburg advised his clients that they could avoid the harmful influences of the planets by constantly moving from place to place and changing their food and drink in harmony with favourable stars.[1] In this way, he told them, they could cheat death and live forever. We can imagine the endless game of hide and seek through which these unfortunates tried literally to escape their fate. One small error in the horoscope, a moment's lapse of attention, and death would be upon them!

THE WONDERS OF AMERICA

At this time the West was also discovering America and travelling round the world, although its travellers were so imbued with ancient culture that they were more willing to believe the Greek philosophers than what they saw with their own eyes. Thus, to the day of his death, Columbus remained unaware of the immensity of his own discovery. He did not believe America had the right to exist, since it did not figure in the imaginary geography of the Ancients.

The Ancients had located legendary peoples and all kinds of other strange things on the edges of the world. At the dawn of the modern age a similar role was attributed to the Savages. These peoples living in the state of nature were sometimes accorded characteristics taken from the imaginary geography and biology of tradition. America was put to fine use in this way. The Amazons (Greek mythology's warrior women) were transported to the equatorial forest (a geographer of the time describes them as 'beautiful, naked and cruel'); they seem to have disappeared in the intervening years, but their memory remains linked to the great Amazon river that flows through their lands. In 1520, at the extreme southern tip of the double continent, Magellan's expedition found the Patagons, a giant people (assessed at between twelve and fifteen feet tall). Subsequent voyages right into the late eighteenth century only served to 'confirm' this discovery (although the Patagons did tend to become a little shorter). In 1610, and rather further north, on the shores of the Bay of Fundy (New Brunswick, Canada), the New England pioneer Captain

Smith had an unexpected meeting with a mermaid – a very beautiful woman, despite her fishy tail. But for a long time the most prestigious of all the lands of marvels was Eldorado; this kingdom of gold, lying somewhere between the Orinoco and the Amazon, filled the daydreams of generations of conquistadors, explorers and adventurers.

Longevity naturally featured among the wonders of America.[2] Amerigo Vespucci, the Italian navigator who gave his name to the new continent, left detailed information on this subject. The fact that, as Vespucci himself admits, the Indians did not know how to calculate years does not bother him; he does their calculations for them. Thus he says he spoke to someone aged 132. The Indians, he says, live for 150 years and rarely fall ill. The mythological sources of this story are obvious (peoples located on the edges of the Earth and 'before history'; 150 years is a classic long lifespan, which we have already encountered on the island of Iambulus). The details that Vespucci provides, however, have a more scientific air. He offers twin explanations for the phenomenon: the particularly healthy air and resulting absence of serious diseases and epidemics (such as the plague, which was terrorizing the Europeans of the time), and the curative powers of the plants used by the natives.

Some America 'experts' raised the stakes. Many of the things we learn are even more surprising, such as the Indians said to live at least 250 years and women as old as 100 breast-feeding their grandchildren.

America also offered what was perhaps the last chance for the fountain of youth. Where else might this miraculous spring be found, if not in a new land where nothing was impossible and imagination turned into reality at every step? Juan Ponce de León, Colombus's former companion who became Governor of Puerto Rico in 1509, heard the natives speak of the island of Bimini, where there was said to be a spring whose water could restore youth – at last a precise location!

With the agreement of the king, who was naturally interested by the prospect, Ponce de León armed three ships and set off in search of the legendary island. It is said that the average age of his crew established a record never seen before on the high seas. Old men and invalids were unreservedly accepted on board as indispensable to the experiment's success. They bathed fervently in every spring they found on the many islands on the expedition's route. Florida was discovered in this way, in March 1513, and initially thought to be Bimini. The Spanish disembarked in several different places and tested the quality of the water everywhere they went, with no spectacular results. The optimistic, tenacious Ponce de León returned in 1521 but, rather than a new youth, it was his death he encountered, in a clash with the Indians.

FOUNTAIN OF YOUTH OR RESURRECTION OF THE DEAD?

Art can sometimes make up for the imperfections of nature. Thus, while proving unfindable in America, the fountain of youth made a remarkable appearance on a canvas usually credited to Lucas Cranach the elder (1472–1553), although sometimes attributed to his son Lucas the younger (1515–1586). Cranach's work was inspired by both religion and classical mythology (he sometimes combined the themes) and in this respect is typical of the Renaissance synthesis.

Der Jungbrunnen (*The Fountain of Youth*) is dated 1546 and shows a kind of swimming pool towards which many old women are rushing, using a wide variety of forms of transport (one on a horse, most in chariots, another carried on a litter and the poorest in a wheelbarrow). On reaching the water's edge the ladies undress, revealing bodies that are not very lovely to look at, jump into the water and come out the other side entirely rejuvenated. Gone are

Lucas Cranach the Elder, *The Fountain of Youth*, 1546, oil on wood.

the wheelbarrows and litters: now knights in ceremonial dress offer their hands to the beautiful, naked young women. Once they are properly dressed, everyone sits down to a celebratory feast.

Cranach's picture is simply the most refined expression of a subject that was frequently depicted in art and literature. His compatriot Hans Sachs (1494–1576), one of the period's most representative German poets, praised the fountain of youth in his poem *Der Jungbrunnen*, written in late 1545, around the same time that Cranach was working on his painting and setting a similar scene. The only difference is that, in Cranach's work, there are only old women to be seen, whereas Sachs's crowd seems to be male. From every nation and every social class the decrepit old men come running: monks, priests, knights, servants, town-dwellers, peasants and artisans rush to the miraculous water. The result is well worth the effort: after bathing for an hour their apparent age reduces from 80 to around twenty. Unfortunately though, the honest Hans Sachs admits, it is only a dream.[3]

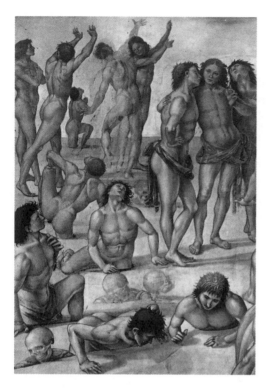

Luca Signorelli,
'The Resurrection', detail
from a fresco of the Last
Judgment, 1499-1504,
in the San Brizio chapel,
Orvieto Cathedral.

Although tempted by youth and cultivating the beauty of the body,
the period was nevertheless haunted by death and obsessed by a thousand real or imaginary perils (from war and plague to witches' spells
and the end of the world). The absolute end remained the Last
Judgement, inspiring both terror and hope and believed by some to be
very close. The Resurrection was also a means of rejuvenation, the ultimate solution, absolute and definitive. Its only disadvantage was that
one had to die and risk the pains of Hell in order to attain it. A striking
fresco depicting the *End of the World* was painted by Luca Signorelli
(*c.* 1445–1523) between 1499 and 1504 on the walls of the chapel of S.
Brizio in Orvieto Cathedral (in the Umbria region, north of Rome).
One segment shows the moment of the Resurrection. Skeletons are

emerging from the Earth and donning their fleshly coverings once more, to appear as young men and women of astounding beauty.

A comparison of Cranach's painting and Signorelli's fresco seems to me highly illuminating. For these two represent the two sides of the Renaissance with its two projects that complement rather than contradict each other.

THE SECOND BACON: *pore-closing and purgation*

The name Bacon recurs in the history of the quest for longevity. Three-and-a-half centuries after the turbulent Franciscan it was marked by a second man of the same name. Philosopher, politician and Chancellor of England under James I, Francis Bacon (1561–1626) firmly believed in the perfectibility of science and the improvement of the human condition, including life expectancy. He published a book on the subject, which received a great deal of attention. It was published in Latin in 1623 as *Historia vitae et mortis* (reprinted five times before 1712), an English translation followed in 1638 (*History of Life and Death*) and a French version in 1647 (*Histoire de la vie et de la mort*). We are in the habit of regarding Bacon as an innovator, principally in the history and philosophy of science. Where longevity and medical knowledge were concerned, however, he was more of a traditionalist. He always refers to the authority of Hippocrates, Galen and Avicenna, adopting, in relation to longevity, their doctrine according to which the proper functioning of the organism chiefly depends on the balance established between the 'humours'. He also believes, like Galen, in the manifestation of a 'vital spirit' that imbues and underlies all material structures.

On the basis of these principles Bacon constructs a simple, effective theory. According to him the spirit is kept in the solid body by force. The body must therefore be very hard and its liquids sufficiently 'thick' to serve as barriers to the spirit, preventing its escape. Everything must work to 'solidify' the organism and 'block' its openings. The pores in particular should be closed by means of cold baths and rubbing with oil. The Irish know all about this; they sit by the fire and rub themselves with oil or old butter. It was just such treatment that enabled the Countess of Desmond to live more than 140 years. However, one must be careful not to rub too violently, because this might let the spirits out instead of keeping them in.

There is another disadvantage: blocking the pores to prevent the spirits escaping also prevents loss of sweat, with the result that the body remains loaded with excrement. The best way to eliminate this damaging surplus of humours is to perform 'gentle purgations and enemas'. Nothing could be better for the health than a good purging shortly before a meal. Frequent, indeed daily, purging is best of all. For those who maintain such a regime excessive temperance on the Cornaro model becomes unnecessary. Such frequent elimination makes it permissible to consume, and even to enjoy 'large meals' every now and then. Opium and powdered gold are also recommended, as indeed are pearls, coral and certain kinds of wood, all of which thicken the blood and other bodily fluids.

Bacon had a well-developed penchant for systems; in this he was a forerunner of Descartes, Newton and the Enlightenment. Everything in his work is presented in the context of a rigorous typology. He knows that the people of the north live longer than others, as do island-dwellers. He also knows that a hairy torso indicates poor life expectancy, while those with hairy legs are conversely more likely to reach an advanced age; strangely it seems there is no connection between baldness and longevity. Bodily proportions are, however, worthy of particular attention: it is a good sign to have a rather short torso and long legs. Nor are the buttocks neglected, small ones providing the most favourable indication where life expectancy is concerned.

In this way Bacon constructs a 'perfect science' using outdated knowledge, a fairly common approach at the time, when scientific thinking was still in its infancy. The early days of the modern age were decidedly less modern than we might like to think. In 1683 the 'first' Bacon treatise appeared in London, translated from Latin with the title *The Cure of Old Age and Preservation of Youth*. The publisher, Dr Richard Brown, member of the Royal College of Physicians, provided the 400-year-old text with a profusion of notes, intended to clarify the author's recipes, including the many for elixirs of life. This treatise seems to have been regarded as up-to-date. People spoke the same language from one century to the next, so that dialogue between the generations remained uncomplicated. Before the iconoclasm of the Enlightenment there were no major shifts in scientific approaches. However, during the same period the spirit of systematization and confidence in the powers of science made steady headway. This development prepared the ground for the Enlightenment, in other words for an infallible science that could run parallel to or replace religion.

PEASANTS AND PHILOSOPHERS

He who looks is bound to find. In response to calls from all sides, the centenarians eventually answered, led by two highly remarkable British men.

The absolute record went to a certain Henry Jenkins, who died in Yorkshire in 1670. In 1513, at the age of twelve, he had taken part in the Battle of Flodden Field. Several documents certified the later events of his life. Born in 1501 he had really lived 169 years. His last occupation was that of fisherman and he would swim vigorously in the sea aged more than 100.

His compatriot Thomas Parr was a little younger when he left this world, but his case impressed the scientists, eventually becoming a symbol of longevity and guarantee of its 'feasibility'. The following is a biographical note written in the late eighteenth century:

> He was a poor peasant, obliged to live by the work of his hands. At the age of a hundred and twenty he made a second marriage to a widow, who lived for twelve years with him and who assured that she never noticed his age. Until the age of a hundred and thirty he never relied on anyone to carry out all the tasks that his farm required, not even when it came to threshing the wheat. It was only a few years before his death that his memory and sight began to weaken; yet he retained to the end his faculty of understanding and the use of his reason. He was a hundred and fifty-two when the king, having heard about him, wanted to see him and had him brought to London. This journey probably shortened his life, for he was treated with such magnificence, and suddenly transported into the centre of a way of life so different from that which he had led until then, that he died shortly after his arrival in the capital, in 1635. He had lived a hundred and fifty-two years and nine months and seen nine kings succeed each other to the throne of England.[4]

What happened after that was no less remarkable. William Harvey, the most famous doctor of the period, undertook the autopsy. Everything was in a perfect state; there were no lesions, no sign of ageing. Thomas Parr died in excellent health.

He had, in a sense, committed suicide by accepting treatment that was the complete opposite of Cornaro's principles and which, in any case, clashed with his usual regime. He died, quite suddenly, from having eaten too much.

Longevity champions were mostly men (conforming to an old tradition) from the lower social classes (living closer to nature). Representatives of other categories include Katherine Fitzgerald, Countess of Desmond, who was born in 1464 and died in 1612. This means she would have lived 148 years; not as long as Jenkins and Parr, but not bad all the same.

The practice seems to have been in better shape than the theory. Jenkins and Parr were contemporaries of two great philosophers, Francis Bacon and René Descartes, who were also interested in finding ways to prolong life. We have already explored Bacon's recipes. Did he apply them to himself with sufficient rigour? Whatever the case, the fact remains that he died in 1626, at the age of 65. Descartes meanwhile was quite simply obsessed with longevity. His medical researches were all focused on this goal. In a letter dated October 1645 he wrote, 'The preservation of health has always been the principle aim of my studies'. In another letter, written in January 1638, he precisely states that he expects to live beyond 100 years. Unfortunately he remained discreet about the methods he had devised to reach such an age. Perhaps the desire was enough in itself. In 1649 the philosopher was invited to Stockholm by his admirer, Queen Christina of Sweden. Of course he spoke to her of – among other things – the prolongation of life (and, in particular, his own). He had not given enough thought to the cold in Stockholm, however, which proved stronger than his determination to live long. He died in the Swedish winter (in February 1650) aged 54.[5]

The scores are impressive: 169 and 152 against 65 and 54. Yet who today remembers Jenkins and Parr? Though ignorant of philosophy they were doctors of longevity and could have taught the philosophers their art. However, their teachings were not entirely lost; they would become integrated into the modern approach to longevity.

The scientists thought they had scored a point – and a decisive one at that – with the new technique of blood transfusion. Although revolutionary, the procedure was, as is often the case, grafted onto old fantasies. Blood as a life principle and young blood as a means of rejuvenation are part of an archetypal store of beliefs and symbols. Rumours and legends tell of abducted children and sinister old men trying to regain their youth by stealing their victims' blood. I have already mentioned the bath in children's blood that was proposed to heal Constantine. In the reign of Louis xv of France, Paris was buzzing with rumours of children who mysteriously disappeared; it was said that the king was bathing in their blood.[6] More recently Nicolae Ceauşescu and his wife, the rulers of communist Romania, were suspected of resorting to the same treatment or, in another version, to transfusions of young blood. The extreme manifestation of this mythical impulse is vampirism; vampires manage to survive their own death by drinking the blood of their victims.

At first, starting in 1650, the transfusions were practised on animals (the first success belongs to the English doctor Richard Lower). The first attempt on a man was carried out in Montpellier by Jean Denis in 1667, using lamb's blood. Until the nineteenth century only animal blood was considered for use, with no concern for any possible incompatibility. The principle was apparently simple: an infusion of young, healthy blood should heal and rejuvenate the organism. The results say it all: the process produced far more victims than centenarians.

The doctors gave up; however the hope remained strong. Very late in the eighteenth century C. W. Hufeland, a doctor specializing in longevity, decided it would be a good time to try further experiments, on the following grounds:

No one has dared to try transfusion again; however it has been entirely successful [. . .] in animals. It should thus not be proscribed unreservedly; [. . .] the foreign blood it would introduce into our veins would soon be converted into our own blood; [. . .] it could, in this way, contribute to rejuvenation and the prolongation of life.[7]

Transfusion, like the long lives of peasants, is symptomatic of a certain evolution of attitudes. Nature and Science were gradually overtaking the religious and mythological models. Pure country air already seemed more favourable than cold monastery walls, and more accessible than the conditions offered by exotic countries. In other words, it was possible to live a long life without being either a saint or a savage. Medicine in turn seemed to be on the right path to find more practical remedies than the fountain of youth. The age of Enlightenment was around the corner.

4 Reason Works Miracles

The Eighteenth Century

The mid-eighteenth century saw the start of a process of accelerated growth that would change the face of the world. For thousands of years humanity had been progressing by small steps; but now suddenly the West (which had entered a dynamic phase of history already in the twelfth and thirteenth centuries) began to run in leaps and bounds, faster and faster from one generation to the next. This was the beginning of the modern technological and industrial revolution. Henceforth traditional civilization, which was essentially rural and based on manual work, would gradually give way to technological civilization, which is essentially urban and maintained by the work of machines.

For the first time in the history of humanity Progress became tangible. The door to the future was flung wide open and the prospects looked attractive.

Was a God still necessary? Some were already beginning to doubt it. Man seemed adult enough to get by on his own, and perhaps better than he had with divine help. His vocation was to become master of his own destiny.

The philosophers of the Enlightenment launched a merciless combat against the superstitions, fears and irrational hopes of a mystical age they now regarded as outdated. Their weapon was Reason, the new divinity.

The anti-mythological fervour of the Enlightenment had a

rather paradoxical result. The world, nature and history were re-interpreted and put into equations. Yet the human mind cannot escape the temptation of mythology. We are programmed that way. It is precisely our ability to function in the imaginary register that distinguishes us from animals and robots, which remain prisoners of brute reality. Ultimately, 'sovereign Reason' merely reshaped the substance of myth, pouring it into an apparently philosophical and scientific mould.[1]

Let us start with God, who was replaced in his role – and no less tyrannically – by the laws of the universe. Newton (himself a believer) became a kind of god in the eyes of the philosophical elite precisely because he had formulated the universal law of gravity, thereby subjecting the universe to a principle of order. At the same time the 'laws of history' were taking the place of destiny. The physicist Ernst Mach quite rightly spoke of the eighteenth century's 'mechanical mythology', which was summed up in a splendid phrase by the Baron d'Holbach in *Le Système de la nature* (1770): 'Nature acts by simple, uniform, invariable laws. All the errors of Man are errors of physics'.

God was no longer permitted to work miracles, but Nature was. Some of the new scientific and philosophical myths scarcely concealed their traditional mythological sources. Thus the 'noble savage' (a theme highly prized by the philosophers), preferably living in the paradisaical setting of the Polynesian islands, is clearly a new version of the myth of the golden age in the lost Paradise. The planets were starting to become inhabited by extraordinary peoples (the ancestors of today's extra-terrestrials) who were simple extensions of the extraordinary inhabitants of the edges of the Earth, now becoming increasingly implausible as the exploration of the Earth itself was almost complete.

One priceless example is linked to the theory of the humours and temperaments so often mentioned here. As we have seen, things were grouped in fours: four elements, four humours, four temperaments. Linnaeus, the great classifier of nature during the Enlightenment period, took up this idea, counting four continents (Australia was missing, being as yet unexplored), four human races, each strictly corresponding to one of the four continents, and, of course, four temperaments, each corresponding no less strictly to one of the four races (the European sanguine, the Asiatic melancholy, the American Indian choleric and the African phlegmatic). This classification tells us a great deal about Reason's role in the perpetuation of mythology.

REASON AND MYTHIC SENSIBILITY

The above observations have three consequences for approaches to longevity:

1. The decline of the hereafter automatically increases the value placed on physical life. It becomes increasingly important to live long and healthily.
2. Science, Progress and the Future seem capable of supplying human perfection, including a significant increase in life expectancy.
3. Extreme, and indeed mythical, cases of longevity are far from being rejected out of hand. As long as there is some kind of natural explanation (and even no explanation at all), no one objects. There is even a fashion for what we might call 'worldly' miracles, perhaps compensating for the growing scepticism of the elite in relation to religious miracles.

The more pragmatic were content to organize their natural spans in the right way, as Cornaro's posthumous career reveals. Few writers are lucky enough to enjoy a new spell of popularity two centuries after their death; such, however, was the destiny of our Venetian. The first English edition of his book is dated 1634 and the first French edition 1647. Significantly these publications coincide with similar concerns manifested in the same period by Bacon and Descartes, but all in all they represent a rather tardy reception, almost a century after the publication of the Italian original. Cornaro's European career proper did not start until after 1700. The Bibliothèque Nationale in Paris records eight French editions between 1701 and 1785. The English editions are harder to count: there were dozens and dozens of them. More than just a bestseller, this was an obsession.

Cornaro had his detractors as well; an *Anti-Cornaro* was published in Paris in 1702, criticizing the strict diet he advocated. The trend was to recommend a slightly less excessive moderation. Yet partisans, critics and opponents were all agreed when it came to the ultimate goal of enjoying the benefits of life for as long as possible.

In reality the Cornaro variant was the least ambitious of methods for attaining longevity, having no whiff of mythology about it. The entrance of the immortals was far more spectacular.

A mysterious figure caused a sensation in Paris around 1750. His name and origins were unknown, but he had come from Germany and called himself the Comte de Saint-Germain. What made him special was that he was immortal. He would pour out his memories of the days of Charles v (ruled 1519–56) or François i (ruled 1515–47) to anyone who would listen. Sometimes he would go a little further and become a contemporary of Christ, one of the guests at the wedding in Cana. He made a great impression in French high society, including, and in particular, Louis xv and Madame de Pompadour, who found his company enchanting. He was even noticed by Voltaire, who, in a letter of 15 April 1758 to his friend Frederick the Great of

Prussia, mentions this man 'who does not die and who knows everything'.

Voltaire's attitude on this matter seems to me to be particularly prudent. This intransigent opponent of all prejudice and superstition, an ironist who ridiculed every word in the Bible, had nothing to say about such a case of immortality. At the time he was moreover skating around the same subject in his philosophical novel *Candide* (1759), whose hero, in the course of his peregrinations, arrives in the land of Eldorado, where he meets an old man in remarkably good health for his advanced age of 172.

Then the immortal count disappeared (no one dares say he died, although some give 1784 as the date of his death). His place did not remain empty for long; his fantastic tales were followed by no less fantastic treatments. The German doctor Franz Mesmer (1734–1815) used 'animal magnetism', a fluid he claimed to be able to tap and use to cure the sick. He likewise established himself in Paris, where, around 1780, he caused a sensation with his 'magnetic' sessions. The rather more traditionalist Italian adventurer Cagliostro, alias Giuseppe Balsamo (1743–1795), also moved to Paris and was received in the highest society, where, like the Comte de Saint-Germain, he extolled the virtues of an elixir of life.[2]

The astounding success of these three figures is worthy of attention. They were received into the centre of a small, sceptical and libertine world that had, in principle, rid itself of prejudice. These people who pretended to believe in nothing at all, except, to some extent, in philosophy and science, were ripe to be caught in any trap that a person of speculative intelligence could set. Because they believed in nothing, they were ready to believe anything.

It would seem that reason does not bring wisdom. The cultivated people of the eighteenth century proved no less predisposed towards mythology than their 'ignorant' counterparts in the pre-scientific world. For Reason and Science nothing is impossible, any more than it is for religion.

The real scientists did not of course go down this path. Yet the extreme cases mentioned above attest to the survival of a 'mythical sensibility' that we find, if in attenuated form, at every level. Naturalists and doctors sought to use the arguments of science to define the natural length of a human life and, with this in mind, to propose means that might assist people to live out this span to the very end. For these men too the proper duration of life was noticeably longer than ordinary life expectancy, with the more optimistic going almost as far as the Comte de Saint-Germain. They felt they were reaching entirely new conclusions; yet in reality they were merely restating the archetype, using more or less new arguments to repeat all that had long been believed on the question of longevity.

BUFFON'S FORMULA

The lowest profile was adopted by the Frenchman Georges-Louis Leclerc, Comte de Buffon (1707–1788), who set out his ideas on the matter in his *Histoire naturelle*, published from 1749.[3] Buffon did not believe that the feats of longevity recounted in the Bible were repeatable. He was perfectly willing to admit that man had lived over 900 years in those days (if not out of pure conviction then at least to avoid trouble); however, such an unusual life expectancy could be explained by no less exceptional physical conditions.

At that time the world was just beginning and lacked cohesion: 'The surface of the earth must have been far less solid and compact in the earliest times after the creation.' Matter was thin and supple, and the same was true of the human organism – especially the bones and muscles – and of food. This explains why the first men were giants and above all why they had such a long life expectancy. The organism matured and aged more slowly. Then, gradually, matter firmed up. Buffon hypothesizes 'that the lifespan of man gradually diminished as the surface of the earth became more solid through the continual action of weight'. By King David's day the process was complete; matter and man had already reached the balance we find them in today.

It is like listening to St Augustine transposed into modern scientific language. Methuselah was still Methuselah, but scientifically explained in a little masterpiece of rationalism reworking elements of the traditional imagination.

While biblical longevity was given scientific support, the same demonstration restricted current longevity to far more modest limits: 100 years, 90 at the least, with a few exceptions, on which Buffon does not linger. In fact 100 years was not so bad, given real life expectancies, assessed for the period as less than 30 years. The only person of any fame to have respected Buffon's instructions to the letter was Fontenelle, who died in 1757 at the exact age of 100. As for Buffon himself, he died in 1788 aged 81 – a fine age, but a little below the 'natural' span.

In principle everyone had a democratic right to 100 years. It was enshrined in the laws of nature. This being so, there was no point in following Cornaro's example: each constitution, each temperament to his own way of life. Of course the weak should take good care of themselves, but why should such an attitude help people full of vitality? 'It may be necessary for the body to use all its forces . . . What is then to be gained by diet and privation?' One could, at the least, live according to one's heart and truly enjoy life. On the other hand there was no possibility of 'breaking through the ceiling'. Any hope that one might lengthen one's days by means of remedies was purely imaginary.

'Panaceas, whatever their composition, blood transfusions and other methods that have been proposed to rejuvenate or immortalize the body, are at least as much of a chimera as the fountain of youth is a fable.'

Geographical and social surroundings and food also seem unimportant:

> When we think that the European, the Negro, the Chinese, the American, men who are policed, the savage, the rich man and the poor, the dweller in the town or the country, so different one from the other in every other way, are similar in this respect and each has only the same amount, the same span to travel from birth to death; that differences of race, climate, food, commodities have made no difference to the length of life . . . we see all the more clearly that the length of life depends neither on habits, nor manners nor the quality of our food; that nothing can change the laws of mechanics, which determine the number of our years.

'The laws of mechanics, which determine the number of our years' – what a wonderful phrase. Man is a machine built to a single patent, in hundreds of millions of examples. Encouraged by Reason, physics was beginning to organize things; it could no longer tolerate the anarchy that had hitherto characterized the pyramid of ages.

Since, it seems, not all men die at the age of 90 or 100, Buffon did accept a certain degree of flexibility, due to 'excesses of food' or 'over-strict diets' (Cornaro's friends take note) and perhaps also to air quality (mountain air was recommended). However, the impact of these factors is regarded as very secondary. The inevitable conclusion is that 'Man, when he does not die of accidental maladies, lives 90 or 100 years everywhere'.

Since mechanics rules, this span can be expressed in terms of an elementary formula. Taking an idea of Aristotle's – for there is nothing new under the sun – Buffon notes the existence of a precise relationship between the organism's growth and life expectancy: 'the total length of life can be in some way measured by that of the time of growth'.

In the last two centuries this discovery has continued to play a major role in the debate on longevity. For what could be more attractive: it is simply a matter of multiplying the number of years needed for growth by the number that expresses the stable relationship between the latter and life expectancy.

In the days of the patriarchs puberty continued until the age of 130 – this is something on which Buffon seems well informed. Multiply this number by seven and you obtain 910 years, a result expressing life expectancy at the time. Today puberty occurs around the age of fourteen. Multiply by seven again: the resulting 98 years, almost 100, express the life expectancy of the man of today.

The calculation itself presents no difficulties; less certain are the two numbers to be multiplied. Buffon seems to hesitate between several different ages to mark the limits of growth: 'Man grows in height until the age of sixteen or eighteen, and yet the full development in size of all parts of the body does not end until the age of 30'. So here is a new constant: 'Man, who takes 30 years to grow, lives 90 or 100 years'. So should we take fourteen, sixteen, eighteen or 30 as the basis? Should we multiply fourteen by seven or 30 by three? Why not multiply 30 by seven, thus gaining a further 100 years?

Buffon's successors, unhappy with an implacable barrier blocking the route somewhere around the 100-year mark, revised his calculations to make them perform better.

One decisive step was taken by the Swiss naturalist, physiologist and poet Albrecht von Haller (1708–1777). His *Elementa physiologiae corporis humani* ('Elements of Physiology', published 1757–66) exerted a notable influence on the medical theory and practice of the Enlightenment. While Buffon wasted little time on the great centenarians, whom he regarded as insignificant exceptions, Haller turned his attention to precisely this subject. He identified 1,000 cases of people who had lived between 100 and 110 years, 60 cases between 110 and 120, 29 between 120 and 130, fifteen between 130 and 140, six between 140 and 150 and one case – that of our old acquaintance Jenkins – of death at the age of 169. It would seem that Buffon had underestimated the importance of this category. Exceptions they may be, but significant all the same, proving the capacity of human nature to go beyond – indeed far beyond – the 100-year mark.

From these statistics Haller drew the curious conclusion that man is the creature that lives longest, longer than any other animal. He even added that the extreme limit of man's life is no less than 200 years, exactly twice the figure accepted by Buffon. All this was justified by a table of data showing only one individual who had lived to be over 150.

On the basis of these different cases and statistics the systematizing spirit of the Enlightenment proceeded to manufacture the science of macrobiotics. Its birth was registered in 1796, when the German doctor Christoph Wilhelm Hufeland (1762–1836) published a work entitled *Makrobiotik, oder die Kunst das menschliche Leben zu verlängern* (in English: *The Art of Prolonging Life*; in French: *La Macrobiotique; ou, l'art de prolonger la vie de l'homme*). Hufeland had a remarkable career, teaching at the universities of Jena and Berlin and becoming physician to the king of Prussia;

more remarkable still, however, was the career of his book and the theories it contained.

For Hufeland had, unawares, given new life to the myth of the golden age. His aspiration was not to invent a different man, but simply to enable modern man to experience the advantages enjoyed by his ancestors in the days when the world was young:

> When its inhabitants, wild, simple and hard-working, true children of nature, were still only shepherds, hunters or farmers, they ordinarily reached a very advanced age; however as soon as they broke faith with nature and were spoiled by the excesses of civilization, indulging themselves more with luxurious pleasures, their life grew appreciably shorter. Any revolution that would return a people of advanced civilization to a state closer to nature would enable them to attain the natural length of life, as in the past.

Let us note the word 'revolution'. The date is 1796 and what the Revolution proposed was precisely to re-establish a natural equilibrium in the life of society and that of the individual.

But precisely what was the famous 'natural length of life'? Returning to Haller's hypothesis, Hufeland assessed the extreme, ideal or potential limit as no less than 200 years. This was distinct from the relative length, which was determined by particular conditions of biology and civilization, judged to be unsatisfactory. Today's man was paying for the accumulated sins of preceding generations, to which should be added an incalculable number of illnesses and accidents. Thus it was impossible now to envisage a life expectancy of a century and a half or two centuries.

But there is no cause for despair. If man is programmed to live 200 years, the obstacles will eventually be overcome and he will be assured his normal slice of life.

The scientific arguments that allowed Hufeland to state this certainty were not very numerous, but they seemed weighty enough. First, of course, were Haller's statistics. If there were people capable of living 150 years, and even 169, in a poor biological and social environment, it was reasonable to risk the assertion that there was nothing exaggerated about a natural length of two centuries – quite the reverse.

Then there was the famous autopsy carried out by Harvey on the body of Thomas Parr. This man, whose insides had been found to be in a perfect state, could well have lived another half-century.

The genealogical data of the Bible had also to be examined and accounted for. Hufeland did not follow Buffon on this point, refusing to believe that man was different in the days when the world was in its infancy. He did not, however, consider challenging holy writ. The only problem to be solved related to the calendar. Some 'experts' already believed that, before the Flood, a year had probably lasted no more than three months, later extending to eight and finally stabilizing around twelve. Consequently what the Bible says is strictly true, with the precision that three different systems of calculation must be used.

This means that in fact Methuselah lived 242 years, slightly more than the two-century limit, which was itself flexible and a matter of convention. In truth the real, if always unavowed, source for longevity experts in the Age of Reason seems to have remained the Bible, which they then adapted to modern scientific demands. Moreover, one cannot help but smile at the rationalist method they employed, since there was no need to wait until the eighteenth century and the Enlightenment to divide the year by four. Pliny and the contemporaries of St Augustine, rationalists in all but name, had resorted to the same strategy long before.

The new 200-year horizon required a reworking of Buffon's calculations. The formula itself was not in doubt, it was simply a matter of changing the numbers. It can be posited in principle, Hufeland decided, that an animal lives eight times as long as it takes to grow. Man needs 25 years to finish growing, which translates into a life expectancy of 200 years. Eight times 25 – yes, it's really true, that makes a total of two centuries.

Thus, using a mixture of statistics, autopsy, the Bible and the multiplication tables, it was demonstrated that man seemed destined to live for 200 years.

CLIMATE, FOOD AND LOVE

Let us stay with Hufeland for a moment, in order to identify a few particular elements of the new science of longevity.

First of all, the geographical location of the phenomenon. Are there any especially propitious regions? It is tempting to suggest those places where official records seem least reliable; this possibility, however, did not seem to bother the longevity experts. Buffon, we should remember, had more or less eliminated environmental influences; for him only the human machine counted. This interpretation fitted well with the spirit of the century; however, the opposing version, which focused on the decisive influence of the environment, fitted equally well. In either case the system functioned perfectly, in accordance with the supreme commands of the scientific laws. For the Enlightenment this was the main thing.

On the matter of environmental influences the tone for the period was set by Montesquieu. According to the theory he unfolds in *De l'Esprit des lois* (1748), the configurations of nations and states, social structures, manners and mentalities could all be explained by geography and, in particular, by climate. In reality this was simply a reworking of an older theory. The main points, including that of the impact of the environment on longevity, had been made long before by Hippocrates.

In this debate Hufeland is closer to Hippocrates and Montesquieu than he is to Buffon. He systematizes the propositions of the great Greek doctor in a manner akin to Montesquieu's geographical and climatic determinism. It is very important – Hufeland explains – if one wants to become really old, to live in a country with a fairly stable climate, which is not subject to extremes of heat or cold, or of humidity or drought. We should moreover distinguish between longevity and 'super-longevity'. The former can cope with differences, as in the case of Germany, where people live fairly long lives. Germans, however, rarely reach a very advanced age, because of the accursed caprices of the atmosphere, which consume their strength and tire their organs.

A cool climate is best and, as a result, very old people are more numerous in high places than in lower regions. However it is important to remain below a certain altitude, as glaciers are not good for the health. The mountains of Scotland are to be preferred to those of Switzerland. The rule is borne out by the Nordic lands, where longevity is greater than in hot countries; however this logic should not be taken to the extreme of a move to Greenland. Excessive cold shortens lives.

Those in a position to choose should select an island. The myth of the island had remained vigorous down the centuries, its most remarkable Enlightenment manifestation being the Polynesian paradise; it comes as no surprise, therefore, to find it turning up in the debate on longevity. On islands, asserts Hufeland – and on peninsulas too – living conditions have always been better than in other regions. People live longer on islands than on continents at the same latitude. It is thus easy to explain the greater life expectancies of the British, and even the Danes, compared to those of the Germans. Sea water has a part to play, being a more effective producer of centenarians than fresh water, to say nothing of still water, which is extremely damaging. This explains why sailors generally live to a very old age. In conclusion, the champion countries for longevity are Britain, Ireland, Denmark, Sweden and Norway.

People do not live long in conditions of either opulence or destitution. An average diet is the most suitable (an upward revision of Cornaro). One should faithfully follow nature and its laws, leading the simple life of the country-dweller, ploughman or sailor. Hufeland also recommends vegetarianism, observing that a great many centenarians have never tasted meat. Physical exercise is beneficial, as is a certain liking for the opposite sex. All the men who have reached a great age have tended to be married more than once, the last time at an advanced age. No single man is ever mentioned as having lived more than 100 years. This rule applies to women as much as to men, Hufeland decides. He goes on to mention the edifying case of a Frenchman by the name of de Longueville, said to have lived 110 years, who married ten women, the last when he was 90 (she gave him a son in his 101st year).

However, in relation to extreme longevity as to everything else, women remain in the background. A paradox could be observed: more women than men reached old age, yet of this privileged group only the men managed to extend their span to the furthest degree. The explanation seemed to be that the balance and softness of women's bodies gave them the advantage in relation to longevity up to a certain point; to reach the extreme limit, however, male vigour was vital.

Man set off alone to conquer a very long life. Well, not quite alone, since women travelled with him, but these were certainly not women of his own age.

So the 200-year standard was set; yet to live it in a state of decrepitude would have been an uninviting prospect. The new magicians of longevity promised a vigorous old age and a new appetite for life, with sexuality – in accordance with the archetype – as one of the major attractions.

Hufeland also notes a natural phenomenon of rejuvenation that occurs at a very advanced age: some old men grow new teeth and hair and throw themselves back into normal life to live another twenty or thirty years. This is certainly most encouraging.

Sceptics need only consider the career of a highly remarkable Dane by the name of Christian Drakenberg. He was born in 1626, served as a simple sailor on the high seas until the age of 91, then spent fifteen years as a slave of the Turks, during which time he suffered the greatest hardships. At the age of 111, thinking it was time to enjoy some rest, he decided to marry and wed a woman of 60, whom he outlived. At 130 he fell in love with a young peasant girl who, as can be imagined, was not interested in his advances. To cheer himself up he tried several other women; however, rebuffed by all, he resigned himself to the widower's state and lived on a further sixteen years. He died in 1772, in his 146th year.

Although it makes an unhappy love story, this tale provides a fine model of the new youth that will characterize the second century of our existence.

ROUSSEAU AND CONDORCET: *from the Golden Age to the radiant future*

Scratch off the eighteenth century's veneer of reason and all that remains is an enormous myth-making impulse, coloured by the notion of the golden age. It is in this light that we should understand Hufeland, in particular relating his ideas to those of Jean-Jacques Rousseau and the Marquis de Condorcet.

Enlightenment philosophy produced an acerbic criticism of contemporary society, comparing it unfavourably to the world of the dawn of time or of the future, or both. The idea of progress was in its infancy, taking the first steps of what was to become a triumphal march. Ultimately this involved transforming the golden age into a radiant future. Humanity was going through an unfortunate phase, but all would be well once it was back on the right track.

The science of longevity dogged the footsteps of ideology. Original Man could only have been healthy and vigorous; it is civilization that has corrupted his behaviour and health. This idea was forcefully expressed by Jean-Jacques Rousseau in his *Discours sur l'origine et les fondements de l'inégalité parmi les hommes* (1755). In his view human beings were formed with a 'robust and almost inalterable temperament', presenting 'all the vigour of which the human species is capable'. Like the animals, Man lived to the natural end of his life. Disease did not exist; it was a by-product of civilization, with its inequalities and excesses such as the excess of work, of idleness, of well-being or penury. The only maladies known to the 'savages' were injuries and old age. This is the natural state of man, which we must try to reintegrate into our own lives, without of course abandoning certain benefits of civilization.

We can see how, although the faces may have changed, the structures persist. The role of the biblical patriarchs and men of the golden race has been taken over by the savages, while philosophy has taken the place of mythology.

The Polynesian islands visited by Captain James Cook (between 1768 and his death in 1779) and by the French navigator Louis-Antoine de Bougainville (1768) seemed to provide striking confirmation of Rousseau's theory. Bougainville in particular, being more of a philosopher than Cook – in other words further from reality – made a major contribution to the image of an insular world, peopled by beautiful, healthy men and women, who lived without a care in total harmony with nature. Diderot, in his essay

Supplément au Voyage de Bougainville, imagined a noble old Polynesian man, still vigorous despite his age of over 90, who taught the Europeans the true secret of longevity, which he sums up in two words: freedom and nature.

For Condorcet the golden age was to be found at the other end of evolution. His project was a sign of the times and, more precisely, the fruit of the French Revolution. In the late eighteenth century the rate of progress suddenly accelerated. The Revolution gave the world a dose of rejuvenation, opening up the prospect of a great leap into the future. None of the values of the golden age, with its primordial coherence and harmony, would be lost. Indeed it was possible to improve on them. Bringing back Original Man no longer seemed enough; he must be transformed, through the invention of a new human being.

Condorcet wrote his *Esquisse d'un tableau historique des progrès de l'esprit humain* ('Sketch for a Historical Picture of the Progress of the Human Mind') in 1793. It was published two years later, after the philosopher's tragic death as a victim of the new times he had glorified. It is the last chapter, dealing with 'The Future Progress of the Human Mind', that concerns us here. In it Condorcet announces a true revolution in the field of longevity. The logic is faultless: in a time of revolution, everything must be revolutionized; in a restructured world of equality between classes and nations and universal brotherhood, human nature must change in its turn.

Progress would manifest itself in both the biological and social spheres. The naturalists had already observed that there was a degree of variability within species – a prologue to the evolutionism of the following century. Social equality would put an end to abuses, to the extremes of poverty and wealth; science, medicine and hygiene would overcome disease, and life expectancy would increase as a result. It all followed perfectly.

At this point Condorcet advances an extraordinary hypothesis: instead of promising the 'new man' 100, 150 or 200 years, he says that no definitive end should be set on longevity, which will constantly increase, in step with the overall rate of progress. Although 'man will not become immortal', the victorious Revolution and excellent new times ahead will apparently offer everyone a real chance to live for centuries.

We should note that man will not become immortal; death is apparently the last traditional obstacle, which Condorcet still respects. We should also note, however, that longevity now has no limits, not even the 200 years granted by Haller and Hufeland.

A WORD FROM FRANKLIN

Benjamin Franklin was also attracted by the idea of an indefinite increase in life expectancy. While Condorcet saw the movement towards the perfect society as the prime cause, Franklin's hopes were more specifically pinned on scientific developments. For him longevity was only one aspect of a world transfigured by scientific discoveries and their applications. Here is a brief fragment from a letter written in 1780 by the inventor of the lightning-conductor:

> The rapid progress *true* science now makes, occasions my regretting sometimes that I was born so soon. It is impossible to imagine the height to which may be carried, in 1,000 years, the power of man over matter. We may perhaps learn to deprive large masses of their gravity, and give them absolute levity, for the sake of easy transport. Agriculture may diminish its labor and double its produce; all diseases may by sure means be prevented or cured, not excepting even that of old age, and our lives lengthened at pleasure even beyond the antediluvian standard.[4]

In 1793, while Condorcet was sketching out his 'historical picture', across the English Channel an essential work for approaches to longevity, William Godwin's *Enquiry Concerning Political Justice*, was published. Godwin shared Condorcet's goal of human perfection and the indefinite extension of life expectancy. However his methodology is quite different. In contrast to Condorcet's primarily social project, Godwin puts his faith in individuals and their readiness to modify their own nature. He expresses both the individualistic variant and the voluntarist current of Enlightenment philosophy.

Man must learn to use the power of his intelligence to control his biological functions. He must express a positive conception of life and behave in an optimistic, confident manner. The path to 'immortality' involves 'chearfulness [*sic*], clearness of conception and benevolence'. We fall ill and die largely because we regard this fate as inevitable. The best way to attain long life is to believe that we will.

Here we see the most complete expression of the view that everything is subject to sovereign Reason. It is also, however, a secularized version of much older currents that place a greater value on the mind than on the body (present in Christianity – clearly expressed by Thomas Aquinas – and equally in Daoism). Reason has simply taken the commanding place of the soul. This extreme manifestation of the voluntarist tendency continued to evolve; 150 years later George Bernard Shaw would refashion Godwin's methodology. Godwin himself died in 1836 aged 80 – an honourable performance, but a long way from his proclaimed biological revolution.

Godwin and Condorcet met with an opponent in the shape of Thomas Malthus. This is quite understandable: in his *Essay on the*

Principle of Population, published in 1798 (with the explicit subtitle *On the Speculations of Mr Godwin, M. Condorcet, and Other Writers*), Malthus warned of the dangers of overpopulation (setting out his famous theory according to which the means of subsistence increased arithmetically while the population tended to grow geometrically). The only ray of light was that from time to time people would die, leaving room for their descendants. What would happen once people stopped dying? Malthus's discussion moreover remained at the level of principle, since he did not take Godwin's 'mental' method seriously. However Godwin, aware of such potential objections, had already prepared his defence. He believed that advances in agriculture and industry would neutralize the effects of demographic expansion. Above all he thought that the intellectual evolution of the human species would minimize its purely animal functions, leading to less sex and fewer children. In the future, people would live longer and the generations would succeed each other at a slower rate, thus solving the problems of both longevity and overpopulation. In this way Godwin outlined a model that bore little resemblance to the demographic realities of his time, but which now has a certain currency.

SWIFT'S WARNING

All these fine projects were demolished at a single stroke by Jonathan Swift in a passage from *Gulliver's Travels* (1726). During his third voyage Gulliver lands on the island of Luggnagg (100 leagues south-east of Japan). Most remarkable among all the local curiosities is a species of immortals, known as the Struldbruggs (a minority of around 1,100 people). It happens, at random and in any family, that a baby is born with a circular mark on its forehead: this is the sign of eternal life. Gulliver greets this immortality lottery with great enthusiasm; his hosts, however, describe the painful fate of the unfortunates who seem at first sight to be so lucky. After a temporary period of youth, they settle into a definitive and ever more extreme old age, suffering not only from all the usual associated maladies, but also from the despair of knowing they are immortal. They become amnesiac, nasty, envious and unpleasant, living apart from the mortals, who despise them. What they most covet are two things they can never have: the vices of the young and the death of the old. The only advantage granted them by the community, for strictly humanitarian reasons, is the automatic dissolution of any marriage between two Struldbruggs once one of them has reached the age of 80, on the grounds that to be condemned to eternity is bad enough and it would be inhuman to condemn them to the additional punishment of an eternal wife.

Perhaps Hufeland, Condorcet or Godwin would have countered Swift with the assertion that an extension of life also supposed a different distribution of 'age brackets'; anyone living 200 years would still be young at 100 and vigorous at 150. To which Swift would no doubt reply that beautiful dreams do not change reality. Past a certain age we merely advance towards old age, with no possibility of return. Living 'forever' simply means living in a state of old age.

These opposing positions remain unreconciled in the present-day debate on longevity.

5 The Age of the Scientific Utopia

The Nineteenth Century

In intellectual terms the nineteenth century was the century of science; economically speaking it was the century of industry; socially speaking it was the century of the bourgeoisie. (Of course this description applies to the West, notably its most dynamic structures and dominant values; moreover, religion held its ground more firmly than the Enlightenment philosophers would have believed, traditional rural society survived, although diminished in size and importance by the industrial society, while the proletariat sought to make its own challenges to the bourgeoisie.) The rapidly expanding West managed to establish a radical distinction between itself and the rest of the world; it also cut off its own past and set itself up as the unrivalled master of the planet.

Progress was at its zenith, both as a real process and, more importantly, as a symbol; it had become a true religion. This was perhaps the most optimistic of all historical periods. The future was fascinating and countless scenarios describe the perfection to come, be it technological or social. Progress went hand in hand with Evolution. With Jean-Baptiste de Lamarck (1744–1829) and above all Charles Darwin (*The Origin of Species*, 1859), evolutionism, which was initially a biological concept but came to be applied to social organisms as well, emerged as one of the most significant scientific achievements of the century. Nature is obviously in no hurry; it has all of time ahead of it; yet the idea that one could help it go a little faster was already making headway. The result would be a different kind of human being, perhaps even a superman.

Democracy, or at least the idea of democracy, was also making headway as a consequence of the American and French revolutions and social change (the parallel development of the middle classes and the proletariat; the greater presence of the 'people' on the historical stage). However, this did not undermine the domination of elitist, discriminatory structures and attitudes. The West (the 'white man') cast a disdainful eye over other races and cultures and the bourgeoisie did the same with 'inferior' social groups, while men remained clearly more favoured and valued than women.

We shall now consider these characteristics as they apply to the subject of our own discussion. In the nineteenth-century context the myth of longevity appears at once secularized, bourgeois, progressionist and masculine, adjectives that precisely express the dominant values of the society and the period.

The myth had become secularized since the challenge it posed now exclusively concerned biological man and his body. Sanctity, which had long been a favourable condition for longevity, was now reduced to mere wisdom, itself enshrined in a set of practical rules in keeping with the time and its social assumptions. Indeed not only had the myth become secularized, it had parted company with the quest for spiritual immortality and, as hopes of immortality faded, was increasingly asserting its value as a compensatory solution. In this way the avatars of the quest for longevity highlight the gradual desacralization of the world. People invested in the life of the body what they had lost in the hereafter.

Longevity was a bourgeois myth because the values it propagated were perfectly attuned to the attitudes of the bourgeoisie, distinct from both aristocratic wastefulness and the indigence of the poorer classes. In its extensive article on 'Longévité', the *Grand Dictionnaire universel du XIXe siècle* (1866–76), edited by Pierre Larousse, recommended to those seeking long life 'a very regular way of life, without the slightest excess, free of excessive work of either mind or body', thereby placing labourers and scholars alike outside the norm. One's sex life should also be entirely regulated; abstinence was not good and nor was extramarital love (not to mention more serious vices).[1] The art of living long merged with the simple art of living, as recommended (if not always practised) by the dominant bourgeois morality.

It was a progressionist myth because science, progress and the future were expected to enable humanity to fulfil its potential. The religion of science so characteristic of the time ultimately removed any notion of impossibility. The scientific imagination moved into the sphere traditionally dominated by magic. All that was now refused to humanity would doubtless be granted in days to come. History is a long process. Man came from the distant past and his career extended into a very long future. He would have the time and means necessary to turn all his dreams into reality.

The golden age completely disengaged itself from the pre-historic period and moved exclusively into the future. Where longevity was concerned there were no more lessons to be learned from savages and primitives; their life expectancy was in rapid decline. Gone were the illusions of the Enlightenment. Western man, the man of the technological age, should stop looking back. His crucial sphere of existence was now the future, a future promising much, among other things in the battle against death.

This did not prevent occasional glances back to the biblical patriarchs and certain champions of longevity, medieval and modern. Such examples could not be ignored, since they were the only 'living' arguments in favour of the project's feasibility. In fact science, progress and the future quite simply appropriated the archetype, reformulating its traditional manifestations.

The myth was masculine in the sense that longevity was still promised primarily to men, an admirable strategy seeking – yet again – to devalue women. The *Larousse* followed Hufeland's argument: 'Women', it says in the above-cited article, 'attain a greater age than men; however the latter seem to provide the most extreme cases of longevity'. While there might well be more elderly women, the 'super-old' were men, driven on by their superior life-force. There is no need to add that this comparison pitted real women against fictional men. The *Larousse* did contain one rather fuller list of female centenarians among the profusion of male records; this was the famous list from Pliny's *Natural History*, still apparently the only available document on the subject, although we are now well into the modern period. On this point at least it seems Roman matrons fared better than nineteenth-century wives.[2]

It goes without saying that a period so interested in the human organism and its perfectibility produced a particularly high number of works on longevity. To make a complete, detailed review of them all would be both difficult and meaningless. I shall therefore offer the reader the data of a corpus that I have studied closely and which seems to me representative of the whole, consisting of the texts published on the subject in France around the mid-nineteenth century. First among them is the work of a statistician, Charles Lejoncourt, entitled *Galerie des centenaires anciens et modernes* ('Gallery of Centenarians, Ancient and Modern', 1842). This was followed by *Considérations sur la durée de la vie humaine et les moyens de la prolonger* ('Reflections on the Length of Human Life and the Means of Prolonging it', 1845), by an aristocrat, Vicomte de Lapasse. Ten years later Dr Léopold Turck published his book *De la vieillesse étudiée comme une maladie* ('On Old Age Studied as an Illness', 1854) and the same year saw the publication of a book by the distinguished physiologist Pierre Flourens (1794–1867), Professor at the Collège de France and member of the Académie Française; his book, *De la longévité humaine et de la quantité de vie sur le globe* ('On Human Longevity and the Quantity of Life on Earth'), had a lasting success, with the fifth edition coming out in 1873. Next on the list is *L'Art de vivre longtemps* ('The Art of Living a Long Time', 1868) by Dr Louis Noirot, and last is *La Longévité humaine* ('Human Longevity', 1873), by yet another doctor, Pierre Foissac. We should also not forget the article in the *Larousse* mentioned above. I shall now give a brief synthesis of what these texts have to say on longevity.

STATISTICS

First the statistics. This science, which was in its infancy, is one of the most characteristic inventions of a century increasingly focused on problems of an economic, demographic or social nature and increasingly concerned with precision. Statistics contributed to an important shift in emphasis away from individual manifestations towards collective structures and phenomena in a kind of democratization of history and the social sciences.

Longevity, which had hitherto been concerned primarily with individual achievements, also took on a structural air, focusing its research on the life expectancies of particular regions, communities or socio-professional categories.

However, statistics was still in its early stages. Furthermore, despite its appearance of 'absolute' objectivity, it was and remains dependent on the ideologies and projects it seeks to illustrate or support.

Lejoncourt saw the figures in terms of a general table, which he presented as follows:

With the exception of parts of India, where there reigns a perpetual spring and men's lives sometimes reach the furthest limits, the land of centenarians is proved to be in Europe, in the regions of the North such as Great Britain, Germany and Russia, while existence is, generally speaking, rather short in the hot climates such as Spain and Italy, with France in the middle [. . .] People do not live as long at the Equator as they do towards the poles, and longer on hills than in valleys and in the countryside than in the town.

The old myths are still present beneath a veneer of statistics. Thus India remains the land of exuberant vitality that it was in antiquity, while England continues to uphold its traditional records. Buffon's universalism is shattered; the science of longevity too expresses nineteenth-century nationalism. Similarly the denigration of other parts of the world in relation to Europe, and of the South in relation to the North, reflects the attitudes of the time. The best of humanity was concentrated in Europe, notably its northern half, and led the march of progress.

What is striking in Lejoncourt's table is the profusion of centenarians, a plentiful species whose numbers were rapidly growing. Even Spain, whose inhabitants apparently died young, manages a long list of individuals aged between 100 and 120. In England one person in every 3,100 is a centenarian. Yet the biggest surprise of all is Russia, which tops the list over the long term. For two centuries Russian centenarians would offer an argument in support of their country's vitality and power. According to statistics from 1814, one Russian in 245 was a centenarian. In 1838 no fewer than 1,238 people in Russia died at an age between 100 and 165; the accuracy of these figures was regarded by Lejoncourt as unimpeachable, since they had been provided by the Russian Ministry of the Interior.

Dr Turck, however, a democrat and apparently less impressed by the Ministry, offered an explanation for the statistical mystery of the Russian centenarians, which seemed to him to have more to do with culture than biology:

> . . . in Russia, in order to preserve their workers by ensuring that the greatest possible number avoids recruitment into the military, the landowners give a man's name to his son and grandson, destroying the birth certificates, so turning the three men into one and the same person in the eyes of the higher authorities.

Dr Turck was a man of progress, who did not go looking for his examples in the Russian empire; he left that to the twentieth-century men of progress.

When it comes to statistics classified by profession, the prize for longevity is unanimously awarded to the clerics. Lejoncourt regards this privilege, once linked to their familiarity with God, as more probably arising from their 'assured, tranquil existence, *il dolce far niente*' (a somewhat irreverent interpretation). Still according to Lejoncourt, the shortest lives are those of the artists, who are perhaps affected by 'frequently breathing in the emanation of colours' (an ingenious scientific explanation).

Thirty years after Lejoncourt, the figures proposed by Dr Foissac prove that statistical science has made progress. This time the statistics are intended as complete, covering every period and a wide range of professions. Rather than highlighting extreme cases, they are designed to shed light on real life expectancies, in other words the average ages reached in the most diverse sectors of society.

The theologians live longest, concludes the statistician doctor, having added up a long list of the ages of popes, cardinals, bishops, priests (Catholic and Protestant), monks and nuns. Next come the philosophers, although here the Ancients are distinct from the Moderns. The former live an average of 84 years and 5 months, while the latter only just manage 67 years and 2 months. The superiority of the Ancients is understandable: for them philosophy was 'a kind of magistrature and religion'. Let us take, for example, the case of Pythagoras, who:

> required husbands not only to renounce their concubines, but also to observe the laws of modesty in relation to their wives; to women he recommended the virtues of their sex, above all chastity; he regarded frugality as the mother of all virtues. To submit to such precepts would surely be to follow the most important rules of hygiene.

In terms of life expectancy, these 'practical philosophers', faithful to their own precepts, even surpass the theologians of the Middle Ages and the modern period. Unfortunately the philosophical average for longevity was lowered by their modern namesakes, who are happy to discuss philosophy at great length but give never a thought to putting its teachings into practice.

The survey continues with scholars: we learn that these people live fairly long lives, proof that study never hurt anyone; intellectual fatigue, a worry to the average bourgeois, was thus eliminated as a cause of mortality. Next came the poets, in the form of a list of 73 names dating from antiquity to the nineteenth century. These people live an average of 62 years and 4 months. The musicians outstrip them by almost a year, with 63 years and 3 months. A similar method is applied to politicians, painters and physicians, the last being a matter of controversy. Dr Noirot stated that doctors occupied 'one of the lowest levels on the scale of longevity'. How could such people be trusted to prolong one's life?

Despite such ironies, Dr Foissac believes he can use statistics to prove that the life expectancy of doctors is quite appropriate: they come out with 68 years and 2 months (still using a sample from antiquity to the present), more than the painters, poets, musicians and modern philosophers.

Farmers are also given a good average (just behind the clerics) and, interestingly, servants also seem destined for long lives. Indeed, all in all, they are in a more comfortable position than their masters, 'associated, but to a lesser degree, with the joys and pains of the family, they share its well-being, without those excesses that the rich are not always capable of avoiding'. Cases of longevity are also noted among beggars. Even some slaves, when well treated, enjoy a similar advantage. Hufeland, in his day, had denounced slavery as a terrible cause of mortality. Dr Foissac seems more inclined to look on the bright side.

It is not worth commenting on each example of ideologically based statistical distortion, all the more insidious since figures are generally regarded with respect. Nothing is regarded with less caution than a set of statistics. This methodology endowed the science of longevity with both precision (whether real or apparent) and credibility.

AIMS

One section of Lejoncourt's book consists of a long list of 'grand centenarians', proving the frequency of the phenomenon and implicitly the feasibility of the project. Among the most remarkable cases are those of a Hungarian farmer who died at the age of 185, having lived 'uniquely on vegetables', and a Polish shepherd, who died aged 188, having never tasted vodka. 'An extraordinary circumstance among the Russians', says our statistician, who tends to get his nationalities muddled. The absolute record went of course to an Englishman, who died in 1696 aged exactly 200. So the 200-year limit is now confirmed by statistics.

Dr Louis Noirot has his eye on the same two-century horizon. He mentions the examples of good old Methuselah (in the minimal variant, divided by four), St Mungo, and a Russian soldier who fought in the Thirty Years War and died in 1801 aged exactly 200.

According to Dr Turck, life expectancy should rise indefinitely from one century to the next (Condorcet's theory again); in the near future he predicts an average of 120 years. This is clearly a cheering prospect, particularly when compared to the average of 40 years recorded in France during the Second Empire.

The most fully developed argument, however, is that of Pierre Flourens. He starts from the famous Buffon formula, which he regards as entirely justified, the only problem being to identify the correct figures to multiply. This is the problem that Flourens sets out to solve, and to which he devoted twenty years of research.

It seems all can be explained by the development of the epiphyses (the ends of the bones). 'As long as the bones are not linked to their epiphyses, the body grows. Once the bones have become united with the epiphyses, the body stops growing; it is around the twenty-year period that this meeting takes place.' So the first figure is twenty, when the development of the epiphyses is complete and growth ceases.

The other figures are no problem at all since, like Buffon (whom he cites on almost every page), Flourens believes that 'everything in the animal economy is subject to strict laws', which are only slightly affected by environmental influences. In accordance with the law, Flourens announces his new improved formula of $20 \times 5 = 100$ years. By remarkable coincidence Buffon's 14×7 and Flourens' 20×5 give almost the same answer. Twenty years of work to confirm Buffon's conclusions. Was it really worth it?

But that is not all. From this starting point, Flourens went on, 'Just as the period of growth multiplied five times gives the ordinary lifetime, so this ordinary lifetime, multiplied by two, gives the extreme length of life'. It would be a hard job to identify the source of this new figure '2'. Ultimately Flourens gets to the same answer as Hufeland, who had, more directly, multiplied 25 x 8 to get the same result of 200.

Flourens concludes, 'A first century of *ordinary* life and almost a second century, 50 years at least, of *extraordinary* life, this is the prospect science offers to man.'

Sometimes, we can only despair of science. For despite twenty years of research, its only role in this argument is to provide an alibi. Science had been manipulated into validating Buffon's waffle and Hufeland's arbitrary decision. Above all it had been used to validate all the main parameters of the archetype: first a span with a ceiling of around 100 years, promised to all; then an extension to a second ceiling of 150 years and, lastly, another extension to the third ceiling, the absolute record of 200 years, hard to attain but achievable all the same . . .

As for Dr Foissac and his predictions, he casts statistics aside to invoke fantasy or, as he puts it, reason:

> It would in no way be contrary to reason or to the laws of the organism for Man, once protected from the illnesses that trouble his harmony and the external violence that damages his mechanism, to live for *several centuries* [. . .] The long view of the patriarchs was more rational, more in harmony with the laws of physiology than the short existence of the men who people the earth today.

We can expect revelations, particularly since Foissac, using Buffon's method of calculation, pronounces himself in favour of a substantial extension of the growth period. He regards the twenty years for which Flourens opts as seriously inadequate; according to him man continues to grow until the age of 30 or even 35. Will he multiply this new figure by eight, like Hufeland, by seven like Buffon, or at least by five like Flourens? No, he settles for multiplying it by three, giving a life expectancy of 100 years, just like that of Flourens. So, 100 years or several centuries? The first seems to define the current state of affairs; for the future let's wait and see.

Dr Foissac does, however, part company from Buffon and Flourens when he asserts that, far from being an implacable given, longevity continually adapts to environmental and social conditions. Civilized Man lives longer than the savage, and the European longer than the Asiatic or the African. Longevity moves in time with the march of progress, which leaves future prospects entirely open.

Overall, the nineteenth-century approach towards life expectancy can be characterized as at once moderate and optimistic. It displays a bourgeois moderation in comparison to the biblical 'ceiling' and other traditional mythical flights of fancy (and even in comparison to some of today's projects). However it remains optimistic in its aim to extend the limit of 100 years into the following century.

Staying in France, the classic book on the future is that of the astronomer and popularizer of science Camille Flammarion (1842–1925). In 1894 he published a vast panorama of the future history of the human species until its extinction (ten million years hence) entitled *La Fin du monde* ('The End of the World'). Here we learn that man will reach his evolutionary peak in 20,000 years time. The planet will be peopled by a single white, small and slender race (largely a synthesis of Anglo-Saxon and Chinese elements). Man will have a larger brain, a refined nervous system and telepathic abilities. Unfortunately there are no surprises for us where longevity is concerned. Our heirs will still be young at the age of 100 and will live for about 150 years. There is little point in travelling through time for so little gain: Hufeland promised more, not to mention Condorcet. In reality Flammarion was simply projecting one of the classic ceilings of longevity into the future. This lack of audacity has a simple explanation: prolonging life was not his first concern. The great popularizer of astronomy believed in the migration of souls and their incarnation on planets. With so many lives and new experiences awaiting us, why cling to life on earth?

But let us return to the year 1842 to meet a most remarkable Frenchman, astoundingly alive among the dry lists and abstract statistics of the centenarians' gallery. This is Noël des Querson-nières, a former steward of the French armies, aged 114 (born in 1728, he died in 1846, at the age of 118). He seems to have fascinated Lejoncourt, who has left us a memorable portrait of him:

A well-preserved old man, looking no older than 60, with a pleasant, full and unified physique. Not only has he no infirmities, he does not even have any discomforts; not the slightest trace of deafness can be discovered in him; his hand is so sure he still shaves himself and his sight is so good that he reads and writes without spectacles.

The gastric juices seem as abundant in this astounding old man as in the most vigorous adult: he requires two kilograms of bread daily. He has three or four meals, the nature and quality of the food being moreover indifferent to him. In the evening, around eight o'clock, he takes a cup of tea with a great deal of sugar, after which he falls into a calm, tranquil sleep around the clock. Never, even in the most rigorous season, is his bedroom or his bed heated; his natural warmth seems, as he says, to be sufficient.

M. des Quersonnières has a sonorous, vibrant voice. He still sings very spiritual little arias of his own composition very pleasantly, and without quavering. He is of average height; yet the vigour of his constitution is such that at the age of 90 he married a young Englishwoman of sixteen, who died in childbirth, leaving him a son.

This is followed by no less impressive details on the prodigious memory and encyclopaedic culture of this most unusual person.

Is M. des Quersonnières the precursor of a new species of human being, of the perfectly healthy man, the 'young centenarian' of tomorrow?

METHODS

Our authors use an eclectic methodology to prolong life, combining such elements as traditional and modern scientific methods, projects for social improvement, moral precepts and culinary recipes.

The most comprehensive work is that of Dr Turck. This republican and man of the left took a keen interest in social problems. His book naturally reflects his preoccupation with social medicine. In order to extend the length of life, the first thing to be done, according to him, is to eliminate the poverty that remains the main cause of mortality. It is therefore necessary to 'multiply work and generalize ease'. Social health is the first key to biological health.

Scientific methods should reinforce policies for social improvement, starting with electricity. This is only natural: the nineteenth century was also the century of electricity. According to Dr Turck there is a great similarity between 'nervous fluid and electrical fluid'. It is therefore possible to use electricity to compensate for the deficiencies of the nervous system, which lie at the source of the ageing process. Experiments had proved that electrical fluid increased vital energy. This force was stated to be 'powerful enough to awaken the sleeping seed of the hair in its bulb, giving it the abundance and colour of youth'. The rejuvenation of the hair perhaps represented the prelude to a general rejuvenation, through the electrical stimulation of the organism.

Never short of ideas, Dr Turck was also interested in chloroform. He suggested using it to plunge patients into a long sleep, a kind of hibernation that would preserve and recreate their biological potential.

It is interesting to note that this man of science and the left also respected the Bible, and not only its spirit but also its letter or, more precisely, its numbers. To divide the age of the patriarchs by four seemed to him a mean trick; he still accorded them almost millennial lives, even though electricity did not exist in their day.

The Bible was also put to good use in a brief dissertation on the virtues of human warmth passed from one body to another: the famous method of King David. In relation to this we learn – Dr Turck updating Galen's recommendations – that there is never cause for despair, even among those for whom touching a young woman is impossible. A healthy child can have a similar effect when applied to the belly, or even a small, fat dog. It's a case of horses for courses.

For Dr Noirot the key to the problem is to be found in sexual morality. If we want to reach an advanced age the first thing we must understand is how to manage sex effectively. The doctor suggests putting a little order into the subject, continually hauled this way and that between the contradictory practices of centenarian bon viveurs and equally long-lived anchorites. Like any self-respecting bourgeois, he ultimately opts for moderation.

Contact with young people, particularly young girls, seems to be beneficial. The prestige of King David apparently remained intact. However, it was important to adapt the method to circumstances and the Nordic temperament sometimes demanded a stronger dose. The great Dutch doctor Boerhaave 'successfully applied this procedure to an old burgomaster of Amsterdam. Only, due to his client's phlegmatic nature, he doubled the dose and had the magistrate lie down between two girls.' Sadly there are no details of the results of the experiment.

Some old rascals carelessly played with sex despite their age, which in some cases was over 100. Here is our old friend Thomas Parr in a very tricky situation. Dr Noirot cites a story that tells how this living symbol of longevity 'had to do penance at a church door at the age of 100 because he had seduced a girl and made her a mother'. Mention was also made of women who bore children at a similar age.

Dr Noirot sweeps away all contradictions and illuminates the subject with three propositions: (1) Centenarians whose sexual health was good practised chastity in their youth, which explains why they kept their precious capacities for longer; (2) Anchorites and hermits owed their longevity to chastity; (3) There is one category of debauchees who invariably live beyond the 100-year limit. These, however, are exceptions who merely confirm the rule that 'incontinence is one of the causes that most shorten life'. The fact that most centenarians are married supports this thesis, marriage assuming – at least in the ideas of the time – 'relative continence'.

An interesting idea seems to emerge. Those who renounce sex in their youth may well benefit in their old age. It would be amusing to imagine Thomas Parr beginning his sexual life at the age of 80.

Lastly, the Vicomte de Lapasse recommends a typically French solution based on good cooking. A native of southern France who liked his food, the Vicomte was a strong opponent of Cornaro. He wanted to live a long life, but without sacrificing the pleasures of the table. Luckily for him, his research backed him up: to prolong life one should adopt the complete opposite of the approach recommended by the Venetian ascetic, 'In my opinion there is nothing more favourable to health than succulent fare; [. . .] a skilful cook is the best of all doctors'. He meant a French cook, of course, since 'the French style of service seems to me undeniably the finest of all'. The path to immortality is through French cuisine.

The Vicomte was an elitist as well as a patriot. His strategy for longevity applied exclusively to the rich. The poor could get by with cruder food, for reasons that could be demonstrated scientifically. The rich require richer food because they burn up more of their own substance than other people. They must make up for the effects of passion and sorrow on their sensitive organisms and the fatigue engendered by study, not to mention the 'stinking atmosphere of the salons'.

The Vicomte did, however, recommend some methods for poorer people, including better working conditions, appropriate hygiene and food that was, if not refined in quality, at least sufficient in quantity.

Each social class had its own path to longevity: but, all in all, the best way to succeed was to be a rich, French gourmet.

Yet some French people understood the value of temperance. One of the better-known names was that of Auguste Comte (1798–1857), founder of 'positive philosophy' and father of sociology. The rational world he hoped to organize (*Système de politique positive*, 1851–4; *Catéchisme positiviste*, 'Catechism of Positive Religion', 1852) would feature both health and longevity. Comte set out rigorous rules for hygiene: 'Above all, physical and mental stimulants must gradually be reduced: no more wine, no more coffee, no more tobacco and, lastly, less and less food, with

Comte deciding, towards the end of his life, to measure out all his dietary rations'. Last of all, no sex ('the most disturbing of all our instincts'), or as little as possible.[3] By these means Comte managed to reach the age of 59 – not bad for a first attempt.

We must confess to being a little disappointed. Where are the scientific methods of which the nineteenth century was so proud? There's a little electricity, but not much else. Most 'experts' just keep rehashing the traditional themes, starting with food and sex (and always with the same arguments for and against; depending on whom you read it is either good or bad to eat, drink or make love). Even when revised down, the proposed longevity remains too ambitious for the methods envisaged to attain it.

MAGICAL LONGEVITY: 'Faust' and 'She'

The scientific project was rather too modest and its unfolding a little too slow to stop the mining of more traditional seams of longevity, rejuvenation and immortality in the world of the imagination. God and the devil seemed to be able to do things more quickly and radically. Although banned from the domain of science, magical longevity continued its career in artistic and literary fiction. This flowering, like that of its scientific counterpart, reveals that the quest for longevity was on good form throughout the nineteenth century. Nothing expresses the human soul so well as fiction.

In this light it is instructive to follow the modern avatars of the famous legend of Faust.[4] The story took shape in the Renaissance; it first appeared in published form in a German version of 1587 (*Historia von D. Johann Fausten*). This was followed by – to mention only the most famous – Christopher Marlowe's *The Tragical History of Dr Faustus* (written *c.* 1590, first edition 1604). For the first two centuries of its career the legend does not mention the theme by which it later became dominated. In the early days it is

Faust with Margarita after his rejuvenation, illustration by Ary Scheffer.

knowledge, wealth and power that Faust is after when he sells his soul to Mephistopheles. There is nothing about youth.

It was Goethe who launches this theme in his first version of *Faust* (written *c.* 1770–75). Here Faust swallows a witch's potion designed to restore his youth and make him fall in love. The definitive edition of the play, including this first part, dates from 1832. For Goethe the hero's rejuvenation ultimately remains secondary in relation to the philosophical meaning of the whole. Nevertheless, his innovation became the starting point of a kind of second life for the myth of Faust.

The transfiguration became complete in 1859, when Charles Gounod composed the music for *Faust*, an opera drawing on the first part of Goethe's play (with a libretto by Michel Carré and Jules Barbier). All that this 'new' Faust asks is to regain his youth and the miracle of rejuvenation takes place on stage. Here Faust becomes, as is only right in a lyrical drama, a young man in love. The myth has become degraded – or at least simplified, with a different meaning. The opera was a brilliant success, not only in Paris but also in Milan (1862), London (1863) and New York (1864). In the eyes of the wider public Goethe was eclipsed by Gounod. What most people know of Faust today is closer to the adaptation than the original text. While such vulgarization might be criticized, in relation to longevity it is a good sign. Of all imaginable solutions the nineteenth century ultimately chose rejuvenation (with notable echoes in the following century, such as, in the cinema, *La Beauté du Diable*, a film made in 1949 by René Clair, from a script by Armand Salacrou). The nostalgia for lost youth appears as one of the most pronounced psychological traits of the modern world; in the case of Faust it even manages to bury the story's other meanings.

We should also mention the attempt by the English writer Henry Rider Haggard (1856–1925) to create a female Faust. His novel *She*, published in 1887, depicts an exotic African setting in which a white queen has won perpetual youth by plunging into the 'fire of life'. At the age of 2,000 'She' still looks like a magnificent young woman. Her motivation is similar to Faust's: her goal is love and her method is seduction. In modern literature 'She' is the prototype of the *femme fatale*. Indeed what better expression than longevity (in the sense of unchanging youth) could there be for the mysterious, disturbing aspect of the eternal feminine?

Youth, love and seduction: the bourgeois, scientist century sometimes reveals glimpses of a romantic soul.

While the Western elite was paying homage to the marvels of science and literature, folklore was still concocting legends to the old recipes, including legends of longevity. Unlike older creations, where the 'core of truth' is hard to find – if it exists at all – more modern productions offer a better view of the process of transfiguration undergone by real events. The following is a curious Hungarian interpretation of the reign of Wilhelm I, King of Prussia (ruled 1861–88) and Emperor of Germany (1871–88):

The Szekely [Hungarian inhabitants of eastern Transylvania] tell how Kaiser Wilhelm of Germany owed his long life of almost 100 years to a potion, the secret of which he alone knew. This magical drink, the inexhaustible source of his robust good health, is a kind of 'water of life without death', which gives him, if not endless life, at least phenomenal longevity and sufficient force to maintain the government of his vast empire and to keep the crown prince from inheriting his throne. The crown prince himself, no longer young and plagued with ill-health, cannot persuade his father to give him access to the magic potion, a few drops of which would cure him of his ills. That which paternal jealousy keeps from the imperial prince is however granted to the Kaiser's two favourite ministers, one of whom is the guardian of his sword, the other of his reason. These two knights go out every day, cheered wherever they go by the adoring people. The knight who guards the sword rides his horse around the town; his companion, who keeps the Kaiser's reason, is carried in a chair. All the sovereigns of the world would like the German Kaiser to give them the secret of his longevity, but they try in vain to drag it from him. The 'old man' always tramples on them by taking over their countries.

Recently the Russian Tsar made such an attempt. At first he thought he could get what he wanted by gentleness; but when this resulted in failure, he was driven to take up arms, soon unleashing a terrible war on the matter.[5]

It is easy to identify the elements that have been combined here. First is the real fact of the Kaiser's advanced age (90 in 1887), then the traditional link between longevity and royalty (particularly in the case of an emperor) and the no less characteristic connection between longevity and power. In folklore terms the Kaiser's near-eternity symbolized German domination of Europe after 1870. Similarly political tension in Europe was reduced to a competition between rulers trying to get their hands on the secret of longevity. Clearly, from history to fairy tale is but a short step.

GRAND CENTENARIANS REJUVENATED

Driven on by the hope of prolonging life substantially, the nineteenth century was not at all keen to reject traditional achievements that offered practical justification to its project. Alongside the French authors cited above we can add at least two Americans whose faith in the longevity of the 'grand centenarians' remained unshakeable. Daniel Harrison Jacques, in his *Physical Perfection* (1859), pleads in favour of moderation on Cornaro's model, mentioning ten 'authenticated' cases of people who lived more than 150 years. A few years later, in his book *Human Life* (1867), William Sweetser, professor of medicine at the University of Vermont, calls on our old friends Henry Jenkins and Thomas Parr, adding a few compatriots to the list, including Joseph Crele, who died in 1866 at the supposed age of 141.

To bring these mythical flights of fancy back down to earth we would do best to return to British soil, which offered highly favourable terrain for both fabled old men and longevity's most stringent critics. The latter's attacks took two basic forms: (1) It isn't true; (2) Even if it were true, it's not to be recommended. The first argument was put forward by William J. Thoms, the second by Walter Besant.

William J. Thoms (1803–1885) was a scholar interested in popular traditions who coined the word 'folklore'. He was thus well placed to appreciate the legendary side of things. He stated his position on our subject in a book published in 1873 entitled *Human Longevity, its Facts and its Fictions.* Jenkins, Parr and the Countess of Desmond are greatly rejuvenated by his study. 'There is no doubt', states Thoms, 'that Thomas Parr was a very old man, an exceptionally old man; probably a hundred'. Thoms also seeks to discredit the idea that peasants leading a healthy, frugal life are more likely to live long lives. The phenomenon is better explained by the imperfections of official records in rural areas.

A DYSTOPIA OF IMMORTALITY

With Walter Besant (1836–1901) we find a kind of repetition of the previous century's 'Swift scenario'. Along comes someone who definitively spoils the party, which was in any case on the point of collapse. Even a century like the nineteenth, which was optimistic overall, was not free of conflicting trends. These became more pronounced towards 1900, as fears grew stronger with the approaching future. Beneath the veneer of the *belle époque*, tensions were growing, giving glimpses of the drama to come. What if science and technology ultimately devoured mankind? What if the best of worlds promised for tomorrow were more like Hell than Paradise? At this time utopia began its slide towards dystopia.

Walter Besant was a prolific writer in several genres who, in his novel *The Inner House*, published in 1888, imagines a dystopia of physical immortality, the supreme achievement of the longevity project. Besant starts from a more favourable premise than Swift, since his immortals do not grow old, apparently remaining at the most suitable age, the men at 30, the women at 24.

The recipe for longevity was discovered by a German scholar at the time Besant was writing his novel. Several centuries later a community of 24,000 immortals are living in Canterbury, a city utterly transformed (strangely the reader is not told what might have happened in the rest of the world). Although people no longer die for biological reasons, there is still a risk of accidental death. This leads to a real psychosis: it would be too stupid to die like that when you are immortal! Every possible measure is taken to avoid fire. People no longer travel (too dangerous) and remain more or less imprisoned in their homes.

Between community members equality reigns: immortality has inevitably led to communism; individualism and the competitive spirit have disappeared. In days gone by men and women were constantly running from pillar to post; they were worried, dynamic and aggressive, trying to get on in life and guarantee their children a good future because they knew their own days were numbered. But when you know you are immortal there is no point being busy. The absolute goal has been reached, so there is nothing left to wish for.

All live in the same way. The houses are identical and all their rooms are the same. Everyone has a bedroom and nothing more. Men and women are dressed identically. People work little and rest a great deal. Above all they eat and drink, the only real pleasures left to immortals. Meals are of course eaten communally, in a great dining room. Love has disappeared, as have children; birth is forbidden as there is no need to replace the generations.

Religion no longer exists (its function was to comfort mortals). No one is interested in art, or indeed in science, except of course in biology and medicine.

The community is governed by a tyrannical council, which is in turn dominated by a paranoid individual who aspires to eternal dictatorship, thereby avenging the frustrations he suffered in the period before the great discovery, when he was just a poor, ignorant boy with no prospects of moving up in society.

Yet, gradually, dissidence takes shape, fed by vague memories of a lost world and by a girl's research in the museum library (she is the community's only adolescent; her birth was permitted to 'replace' someone who had died in an accident). There follows a conflict ending in a split: those who do not wish to give up their immortality, even if it means mindless slavery, remain in Canterbury; those who choose freedom and the happiness of living with the acceptance of death leave to go elsewhere. All things must pass. Life gets its value solely from the existence of death and the succession of the generations.

Besant's originality lies in the way he links and contrasts two myths dear to his time: the biological transformation of man and the 'radiant future' in its communist version. Against these two he sets nineteenth-century individualist liberalism and an awareness of certain biological and moral boundaries that it would be dangerous to cross. Of course his is not a progressive approach; yet it may provide food for thought even to the more progressively minded (particularly after the recent fall of communism and its failure to create a 'new man').

6 Longevity in a Time of Ideologies

The First Half of the Twentieth Century

Even in the mid-nineteenth century, when science was triumphant (at least in the imaginary sphere), the quest for longevity always ran the risk of becoming monotonous, simply proclaiming fine principles. The recommended methods (transfusion, electricity and so on) had lost their novelty. For a long time the same advice had been repeatedly given – in reality it all boiled down to the one great recommendation of moderation. Fortunately everyone practised this virtue in a different way, which lent a little colour to the debate.

But then, suddenly, here was something new. The arsenal of longevity began to expand in the light of the spectacular advances made by medicine in the late nineteenth century and the early twentieth. Henceforth it seemed possible to act on several fronts at once to make the human race better and more healthy.

Two new factors came into play: microbes and hormones. Pasteur and Koch had demonstrated the role of the former in the pathology of infectious diseases (the crucial phase of their discoveries came in the period 1870–90). Now that the microbes had been identified they could be fought. It was even possible, more subtly, to imagine using good microbes against the bad. Longer life of course required the organism to be immunized against its invisible enemies.

Around 1900 the endocrine glands and their secretions, the hormones, set out in their turn on a career that was to influence longevity strategies throughout the twentieth century. It became obvious that many ills and maladies could be explained by a deficit in the flow of hormones. Surely a similar failure might be the source of the ageing process. It was an attractive idea: old age was a kind of illness resulting from a failure of the endocrine glands and curable by treatment with hormones. The fashion's first wave concerned the sex hormones, secretions that were incontrovertibly lacking after a certain age.

Thanks to transplant techniques it should one day be possible to move from simply injecting hormones to transplanting glands from one body to another. In this way the organism would enjoy constant, natural hormonal irrigation, which could periodically be reactivated by further transplants. The result would be not only a longer life, but the perpetuation or restoration of youth. People would be as old as their glands. Hormones became the scientific version of the fountain of youth.

The project to perfect human biology at last seemed to be about to move beyond the planning stage. In this context two scenarios enjoyed considerable prestige: one was eugenics, a science intended to improve the genetic legacy; the other was the global revolution advocated by the communist doctrine, whose goal was the transformation of both society and the individual.

The founding works of eugenics are by Francis Galton (*Hereditary Genius*, 1869; *Natural Inheritance*, 1889) and his disciple Karl Pearson (a professor of mathematics at University College London who, around 1900, proposed that the mechanisms of heredity could be expressed in terms of strictly defined formulas). The eugenicists were worried about the degeneration of the species (or, to be more precise, of Western civilization), which could be imputed to the proliferation of human material of mediocre quality (less successful individuals were more prolific than geniuses). This imbalance had to be remedied by appropriate social and family policies and primarily through the encouragement of beneficial unions (discouraging those burdened by undesirable heredity). So the problem was one of human selection. The issue was not so much to improve the performance of the species as a whole as to concentrate on those individuals with 'good heredity', leaving the rest to fend for themselves. Eugenics had an evolutionist, and indeed 'progressive' aspect, which tempted some moderate socialists (interventionist policy aimed at improving living conditions, social inequalities accepted but contained within reasonable limits etc.). However, its essential influences remain inegalitarianism and elitism and, on both right and left, an interventionist and indeed authoritarian tendency, in other words the rejection of 'laissez-faire' liberalism. The 'dregs' of humanity, a dangerously extensible category, were excluded in advance. The more radical eugenicists advocated sterilizing defective and 'undesirable' elements. Indeed their elimination pure and simple was also envisaged – and put into practice in Nazi Germany. As for longevity, it is notable mainly for its absence. Of course a biologically 'successful' individual had every chance of living a long life; for the eugenicists, however, the social body was more important than that of the individual. It was important to hold on to those gains already made, even gradually to spread them throughout the population, rather than invent a biologically different human being; in other words the eugenicists supported socio-biological purification rather than the transformation of the human condition; their programme was conservative rather than revolutionary.

The biological project of communism, by contrast, was closely linked to its social project. Its aim was to bring about a radical change in the human condition, including life expectancy, and with no forms of social discrimination (once the enemies of the people had been eliminated). Every person would have a democratic share in the 'radiant future'. While the first target of eugenics was heredity, which it sought to put to good use, communism had no interest in biological inheritance, proposing to invent a 'new man'.

Microbes, hormones, eugenics, communism: I shall now describe some manifestations of this new scientific and ideological whole.

ÉLIE METCHNIKOFF AND THE POWER OF BULGARIAN YOGHURT

To take us past the 1900 mark, let us turn to the services of an attractive, if somewhat strange guide. Élie Metchnikoff was at once both a true scholar and a hunter of chimeras – two by no means incompatible facets.[1] He was a Russian Jew, born in 1845, who worked at the Institut Pasteur in Paris from 1887. His research on immunity, particularly the discovery of the phagocytes, or microbe-eating cells, earned him the Nobel Prize for medicine in 1908.

Metchnikoff was a builder of bold theories rather than a methodical laboratory scientist and was not happy simply fighting microbes. His ambition was to penetrate the depths of human nature in order to understand the mechanisms of life and death. His very last battle was fought against death – he lost, like everyone else.

Metchnikoff's preferred lifespan was 150 years. He was very familiar with the Bible. Perhaps he was thinking of the ages of the patriarchs – divided by four. At any rate the long lives of earlier periods as recorded in the Bible seemed to him to be above suspicion. Take, for example, Moses's 120 years: 'the longevity of that distant period', says Metchnikoff, 'must truly have been greater than that of the present times [. . .] We must therefore accept as very probable ages of more than 100 or 120 years attributed to several biblical characters'. Even later records, notably St Mungo's 185 years, are worthy of inclusion in the discussion.

Why had longevity declined? What could be done to push it back up again and, if possible, further than before? These were the questions Metchnikoff sought to answer in his *Études sur la nature humaine* ('Studies on Human Nature'), published in 1903, which saw its fifth edition in 1917, and in a complementary work suggestively entitled *Essais optimistes* ('Optimistic Essays', 1907).

From the outset he asserts that our shorter lifespan and premature ageing is all the fault of our intestines. Dante's Inferno pales in comparison to what happens in our entrails, which are the true empire of putrefaction, ruled by dangerous bacilli. Everything we eat turns rotten – an observation intended not only to take away our appetites, but also to warn us of the unfortunate consequences of our feeding system.

The large intestine in particular is a real scandal: 'a superfluous organ in our organism, removal of which could have happy results'. Even vegetarianism, sometimes praised as an effective method of prolonging life, is of no great use. Food of plant origin goes through a similar process to that undergone by food of animal origin, and all for the greater good of the bacilli of putrefaction, which leave the intestines to invade the entire organism. The result is premature ageing, which is merely the 'poisoning of our tissues by poisons of which most come from our large intestine, peopled by an infinite number of microbes'. Here is the main cause of arteriosclerosis, and of death itself.

What is to be done? Should we strip out the intestines? Such a radical solution would not have dismayed Metchnikoff, who was not one to do things by halves. But in the end he had a better idea.

The name of his recipe seems very ordinary today, but at the time it had an exotic ring: Bulgarian yoghurt.

The centenarians were gradually leaving the West and migrating east. The Balkans welcomed them with open arms, particularly Bulgaria. Apparently Bulgarian peasants lived to a very great age and a considerable number of them passed the age of 100. These same peasants lived mainly on yoghurt. Here was the key to the mystery.

The microbes that produce lactic acid literally hunt down the bacilli of putrefaction. Sour milk in all its forms is thus clearly a miracle cure. Even 'in the Bible sour milk is often mentioned', possibly explaining, if not Methuselah's 969 years, at least Moses's 120. The same product is also consumed in large quantities in Russia; now we begin to see why there are so many Russian centenarians.

Metchnikoff was haunted by the spectre of old age and death; he began consuming sour milk and recommending it to everyone else. Then, to make things simpler, he began ingesting pure cultures of 'Bulgarian bacilli', which, though perhaps less appetizing, was almost certainly more effective. The good microbes fought the bad; the quest for longevity was entering its own scientific age.

In addition to the disorder that reigned in the intestines, Metchnikoff identified two other modern ills: syphilis and alcoholism. The eradication of these two, combined with the powers of Bulgarian yoghurt and, more generally, a healthy, balanced diet, would enable man to return to his natural state and live 150 years. Then things could be taken further, the vocation of modern biology being to 'modify human nature'.

Metchnikoff was also interested in women, as long as they were either young or 100 years old. He was less strict about sex than he was about food and found the proximity of young women stimulating, while their very old sisters offered him rich material for study. It is to him that we owe the interesting observation that 'women more easily reach the age of 100 and above than men'. At last justice was done! Having long been the preserve of men, longevity was at last becoming feminized. The twentieth century had truly arrived.

As a great enemy of death Metchnikoff put his programme into rigorous practice, starting with himself. For twenty years he abstained from all excesses, spurning alcohol and tobacco, feeding himself scientifically and ingesting impressive quantities of Bulgarian yoghurt and bacilli. He died in 1916 aged 71.

DR VORONOFF'S MONKEYS

It is time now to move from the world of microbes to that of hormones, whose marvellous properties we shall verify. We shall begin, of course, with the sex hormones, which at first sight appear to be most involved in the metabolism of age.

The pioneer of this new scientific adventure was the French physiologist Charles-Édouard Brown Séquard (1817–1894), professor at the Collège de France. On reaching a relatively advanced age he treated himself by injecting the products of rams' testes. After one such session the professor had joyful news for his students: 'Gentlemen, last night I was able to pay a visit to Madame Brown-Séquard'. He died shortly afterwards.

Brown-Séquard's method had had its successes (his nocturnal visit), but also presented some failures (the professor's premature death) and needed perfecting. It is now that the remarkable Dr Serge Voronoff (1866–1951), also a Russian Jew, makes his entrance.[2] After studying medicine in Paris he went on to practise surgery in France and, for fourteen years, in Egypt. On his return to Paris he became Director of the Laboratory of Experimental

Surgery at the Collège de France. Between the wars the name Voronoff acquired a slightly sulphurous celebrity. He swept away all the fine principles of moderation, particularly in sexual matters. To economize one's genetic energy might be a good thing, but to supplement it was even better. Long life was not for ascetics, but for those who generously spent their resources, for the good reason that they had more than enough.

Dr Voronoff liked to invoke the great Goethe who, at the age of 80, was still enjoying the pleasures of love. He might also have referred to Victor Hugo, one of whose biographers notes the following detail: 'His notebook begun on 1 January 1885 records eight more performances, the last of all dated 5 April 1885',[3] a few weeks before his death at the age of 83.

Quite frequently it is the hard drinkers and great lovers who live long, observes Voronoff in his book *Les Sources de la vie* ('The Springs of Life', 1933). He goes on, 'men endowed with particularly well-constituted genital glands have a quite exceptional life force'. Physical strength, cerebral fecundity and the preservation of youth all depend on this spring. Eunuchs age prematurely and rarely live beyond 60. It can legitimately be stated, without exaggeration, that a man is only as good as his genital glands.

Once this is established the logic is clear. Man ages because his glands age. To make up for this, the failing glands should simply be replaced with new ones. The solution for longevity lies with testicular transplants.

This principle seemed clear enough and, moreover, such transplants posed no difficulties in surgical terms. There was just one detail to settle: where would the donors be found? It was hard to imagine young men giving up their virility to benefit their grandfathers. The net had to be cast a little wider – but not too wide. Might Brown-Séquard's ram be the answer? No,

The miracles of Doctor Voronoff: Sir Arthur Evelyn Liardet before and after the transplant.

there was a far better source in the form of our cousin the chimpanzee, the creature closest to man.

Thus in 1920 Dr Voronoff began transplanting chimpanzee testicles on to men affected more or less precociously by senility. The result was astounding. Youth returned and, with it, sexual appetite.

One of Voronoff's first patients was an Englishman, Sir Arthur Evelyn Liardet. Two photos taken 'before' and 'after' are more eloquent than any argument. At the age of 74 Sir Arthur was old and decrepit, his face flaccid and expressionless. After the transplant a quite different man looks out at us. From his juvenile appearance he seems 50 at the most, a quarter-century less than his actual age. He proudly displays the 'muscled arm of a young man' and reads without glasses. His sex life had ended twelve years before; now it was busier than it had ever been.

Sadly, shortly after leaving the clinic Sir Arthur departed from life. This was not due to the excellence of the Voronoff method, but to the fact that the incorrigible old dog had taken advantage of his new youth to indulge in alcohol abuse, a former unfortunate habit of his. He died after a fit of delirium tremens.

Not discouraged in the slightest by failures not of his own making, the doctor continued to perfect his method. He and his

'Doctor Voronoff receives the Légion d'honneur' in a caricature in the satirical magazine *Le Canard enchaîné*, 1926. The public is made up of monkeys and men with monkey testicles, already showing simian features.

chimpanzees moved into the Palazzo Grimaldi near Ventimiglia, on the Franco-Italian border. Year after year he had the satisfaction of observing a general improvement in the physical, genital and intellectual faculties of his patients.

Some transplantees even had children following the operation – don't worry, none of them were little chimps. On this sensitive point Voronoff was careful to reassure fathers-to-be: the babies would display 'no simian symptoms'; on the other hand they would show an infusion of simian energy, which was no bad thing. 'While my transplant patients do not father monkeys, by increasing the vitality, the energy of the body, the simian glands produce a particularly robust generation of children.'

Until this point only men had been involved, as the method was primarily intended for them. Voronoff, however, did carry out ovarian transplants (the first in 1923), if with less spectacular results. The women also grew younger, but for the time being to a lesser degree than the men. It seemed the search for longevity continued to respect tradition and favour the male. Voronoff remained optimistic; in the long term he believed he could offer his female patients a further period of fertility.

Still some problems remained. The available number of chimpanzee testicles (or ovaries) was of course limited. How could everyone be satisfied? Benefits remained confined to a small number of privileged people. Furthermore the transplant itself was subject to ageing, and did not generally last beyond six to ten years, so that the operation had to be repeated two or three times. This once again posed the problem of the necessary materials, particularly as each chimpanzee could be used only once. In this world there are too many men, too few chimpanzees.

Yet, such as yet unsolved problems aside, a true biological revolution was in the offing. It was perhaps a great turning-point in human history: one of the doctor's biographers spoke unhesitatingly of a 'miracle' and 'the century's most wonderful discovery'. 'To try to bring man closer to eternity [. . .] is surely to perform miraculous, almost divine work.'[4]

A few more years – eternity could not be far. But the doctor was hoping for more. He reworked Buffon's calculations, multiplying 20 by 7. This was the new length of 'normal' life: 140 years. All that remained was to calculate the number of chimpanzees required for such an extension.

One niggling little detail, however, remains a puzzle. Why did Voronoff not attempt to have a transplant himself? Particularly since, at the age of 70, he made his third marriage to a young woman of 21.

Dr Voronoff's reputation followed a dizzy curve. His fall was as sudden and spectacular as his rise to glory. He made a swift entry into the encyclopaedias and was removed from them at similar speed. Who now remembers his name? His miracles were reduced, at best, to a real but temporary attenuation of the effects of ageing and, at worst, to the illusory effects of a placebo administered by

137

an impostor. Scientifically rejected, his attempt nevertheless has undeniable mythological resonance as the most characteristic modern manifestation of the archetypal relationship between longevity and sexual potency.

DR GUÉNIOT, OR THE ART OF LIVING 100 YEARS

After the heroic, not to say extravagant attempts of the two Russians, we return to a wiser, more pragmatic attitude with Dr Alexandre Guéniot and a system built essentially on the good old methods. Guéniot's ambition is not to attain a lifespan of 200 years, or even 150, but simply the truly accessible limit of 100. This is clearly stated in the title of his book, *Pour vivre cent ans ou l'art de prolonger ses jours* ('How to live a hundred years or the art of lengthening one's days'), the first edition of which was published in 1931. The supreme sign of his wisdom is that the doctor imparted his experience to would-be centenarians at a time when his bet was almost won; born in 1832, he had just celebrated his 98th birthday.

According to Dr Guéniot, man was destined to live 100 years. Since he rarely passes 75 or, at best, 85, the problem is to regain the period between such ages and the natural limit of life. In practice this is an extremely simple operation. The doctor was aware of the more revolutionary methods, but did not seem to place over-much faith in them. He condemns the 'guilty exaggerations' of eugenics in the name of human dignity. He does not dismiss hormones out of hand, but suggests that economization is preferable to the search for supplements that might turn out to be illusory. At 60, or 65 at most, sexual relations should be renounced: 'the genital secretions should be retained for the benefit of the organism that produces them. Diminished simply, rather than dried up, these substances will continue to supply the springs of life. There should thus be no more expenditure, no loss of this physiological stimulant'. This is certainly more practical than transplants, and quite the opposite of Voronoff's method.

In reality nothing beats temperance. One should eat in moderation, drink in moderation and have sex in moderation (while this is still permissible). Vitamins should be consumed, but there is no need to worry, since these substances – whose medical career was just beginning – are to be found in abundance in any rational diet. Lastly one should get as much oxygen into the lungs as possible; physical exercise is crucial, as are walks in the fresh air.

A man from another age lost in violent times, Guéniot appreciates the quiet life and rejects many recent fashions as not conducive to longevity. Fresh air is perfect, but nudism is out of the question, 'since in the natural state we are not covered in fur, feathers or a shell as the animals are' (one might ask whether we are clothed in the natural state). Sport is recommended, except for boxing and rugby, whose effect on the body is more harmful than strengthening. It is also interesting to note that tobacco passes the test without difficulty. The doctor assures us that 'nicotine rarely has bad effects on smokers' and that smoking 'renders a service to many people who have to while away monotonous hours'; 'moreover among smokers we find a certain number of people whom tobacco has not deprived of the pleasure of living more than a century'. In reality this indulgence is a thing of its time. Lastly, although strong alcohol was not recommended, like a good Frenchman Guéniot accepts and indeed recommends a moderate consumption of wine – but not too moderate: up to '60 cl a day for an intellectual worker and 1¼ litres for a man engaged in hard labour'.

The Guéniot method is reminiscent of a modernized Cornaro. It must be said that both men were as good as their word. Each represents a near exception in a field where practice is hard put to match theory: most longevity experts had the misfortune to die young, or at any rate not very old. Dr Guéniot ended his days in 1935, aged 102 years and 10 months.

I do not know that his method would find many followers these days. Times have changed. We would tend to choose sex over tobacco.

Medical advances seemed to guarantee a no less rapid and noteworthy advance in longevity. This was not an opinion shared by Dr Alexis Carrel (1873–1944), awarded the Nobel Prize in 1912 and author of *L'Homme, cet inconnu* ('Man, the Stranger', 1935), a medical bestseller of the inter-war period. According to him, advances in longevity were an illusion. Life expectancy was rising, certainly, but the actual length of life was not changing: 'A man of 45 is no more likely to reach the age of 80 today than in the last century. It is even probable that longevity is decreasing, although the average length of life is greater.'

Carrel noted the ineffectiveness of hygiene and medicine, which had proved incapable, so far at least, of increasing the upper age limit: 'Neither the real advances in the heating, ventilation and lighting of houses, nor food hygiene, nor bathrooms, nor sport, nor periodic medical examinations, nor the proliferation of specialists has added a single day to the maximum length of human existence.' The only notable change was in physical appearance: the elderly still look young, but they are no less old for all that. They will simply have the privilege of dying while still 'young'.

The pseudo-young men who play tennis and dance like people in their twenties, who get rid of their old wife to marry a young one, are vulnerable to softening of the brain and disease of the heart and kidneys. Sometimes also, they die suddenly in their beds, their office or on the golf course at an age when their forebears were still behind the plough or running their affairs with a firm hand.

Such sceptical observations do not mean that man will not prove capable, in the long term, of increasing the longevity of the species. However at this point a further problem arises. Would it really be wise to prolong life?

Longevity is desirable only if it prolongs youth, rather than old age. Yet in reality the length of old age is increasing more than that of youth. In the period when individuals become incapable of looking after themselves they are a burden to others. If everyone lived to be 90, the weight of such a crowd of old people would be unbearable for the rest of the population.

Unlike Dr Guéniot, Alexis Carrel was a supporter of the most rigorous eugenics. In his book he declares himself in favour of forbidding procreation by undesirable elements (criminals, the degenerate) and indeed their physical elimination, for the biological improvement of the species. With a programme like this there is no reason to be kind to those in the third age:

Above all we must not increase the numbers of the sick, paralytic, weak or demented. Indeed, if we were able to prolong health to the threshold of death, it would not be wise to give great longevity to all [. . .] Why increase the length of the life of people who are unhappy, selfish, stupid or useless? It is the quality of human beings that matters, not their quantity.

There is no room for equivocation here. Either the species is improved, making human beings worthy of living longer, or we try to extend the lives of the small group of those who really deserve it. Research should continue, at least for the benefit of the latter. These days such a position would seem repulsive; at the time, however, it seemed 'politically correct', at any rate expressing 'eugenicist' positions that were fairly broadly accepted.

On the directions to follow Carrel has little new to offer, apart from the simultaneous application of several familiar methods. He believed that the transfusion of young blood into the veins of an old person would have beneficial effects. This idea emerged in the seventeenth century and reappears now and again as a tactic for longevity. The Voronoff method was judged excessively simplistic, since 'old age is not due to a single gland ceasing to function, but to changes in all the tissues and to humours'. The organism must thus be renewed on a much grander scale, involving not one but a great many transplants, as advocated by Dr Dartigues in his development of Voronoff's theory. For example, one might replace all the glands of an old man with those of a stillborn child, and his blood with that of a young man. The result would speak for itself. For the moment the phenomenon of rejection prevented such operations, but scientific advance would perhaps make it possible one day.

REINVENTING MAN: *from determinism to voluntarism*

The longevity projects I have just examined, some of them extravagant from a methodological point of view, conversely display a degree of moderation at the level of their objectives. This was not to everyone's taste. Living a sensible life in order to extend old age by a few years can seem a paltry ambition. Things should be taken much further in order to rework and reinvent the human being. Man will be able to achieve purposefully and quickly what nature can manage only slowly and imperfectly. The 'new man' and the 'superman' are not natural products; they are or will be created by the action of man upon himself. They are ideological products along nineteenth-century lines, which ran on into the twentieth century, sometimes in expanded form.

The science and attitudes of this period were deeply marked by two opposing and complementary principles: determinism and voluntarism. The former supposes rigorous, effective action on the part of the environment; the second supposes no less rigorous and effective action by man. The incompatibility between these two extremes is only apparent, for it is very easy to shift from determinism to voluntarism. Once nature can act in accordance with a precise plan and a system of laws, man can act in his turn, according to the same plan and system. All that is required is to find the key to understanding and controlling the mechanism. In this way man can act better and more quickly; for nature sometimes loses its way, but human reason has no reason to stray from the path. This shift from one principle to the other can be regarded as one of the moot characteristic and consequence laden aspects of contemporary history.

At the level of biological evolution – and, implicitly, longevity – the points of departure for this curious tandem of 'determinism-voluntarism' can be found in Lamarck and Darwin. Around 1800, when evolutionism was in its infancy, Lamarck took the view that organisms transformed themselves as a direct result of environmental influence, after which the changes were passed down by heredity. Fifty years later Darwin left aside the transmissibility of acquired characteristics, without explicitly rejecting it, building his theory on the survival of those organisms best adapted to their environment.

Both versions were determinist; each, in its own way, made evolution dependent on environmental demands. Voluntarism adopted evolutionist theory for its own ends in accordance with the dialectic we have already noted, but with an overt or implicit predilection for Lamarck's argument. Indeed it was essential for biological voluntarism to emphasize the transmissibility of acquired characteristics as the necessary condition for the effective creation of new species.

GEORGE BERNARD SHAW: *evolution at will*

Paradoxically, one of the most remarkable specimens of voluntarist biology as particularly applied to longevity is to be found in a stage play. Nothing, however, can be too paradoxical when it comes to George Bernard Shaw. The famous Irish writer is of interest to us here for two reasons: first, he not only theorized but also successfully practised 'long life' in a field where practice is much more difficult than theory – this committed vegetarian died at the age of 94. Second, as a theorist, he avoided the well-trodden paths. When dealing with longevity, as with any other subject, Shaw wanted his work to be original and to say things that would provoke, if not horror, then at least disquiet among the ranks of the bourgeoisie.

His play dealing with the prolongation of life is suggestively entitled *Back to Methuselah* and was published in 1921. Readers have found the text amusing or deadly dull, according to temperament, but it is in any case almost impossible to stage due to its length. What matters is perhaps less the play, a simple illustration of the writer's theories, than the theories themselves, which are expounded in an interminable Preface, itself the length of a short book. It is here that the great Irishman gives free rein to his boundless capacity to say both intelligent and stupid things indiscriminately and with the same accomplished skill.

In going back to Methuselah, Shaw returns to Lamarck, in other words to the transmissibility of acquired characteristics, a mechanism already rejected by modern biology but crucial to the reconstruction of man by small successive modifications. Shaw proudly proclaims himself a 'Neo-Lamarckian'; what he likes about Lamarck, or at least what he believes the theory suggests, is evolution 'at will'. How else can one explain the giraffe's neck? Obliged to reach leaves on branches located several metres above the ground, the giraffe had no choice but to extend its neck: 'The long necks were evolved by wanting and trying', states Shaw. Similarly, 'if you have no eyes, and want to see, and keep trying to see, you will finally get eyes'. Conversely, if you have eyes but do not wish to see, one fine day you will find you have lost them.

This is the only form of evolution conceivable, a conscious evolution that respects the dignity of the creature. It is the complete opposite of the 'natural selection' championed by Darwin, which is a simple, aimless accident from which all intelligence is absent. If this 'hideous fatalism' turned out to be correct, 'only fools and rascals could bear to live'.

What Shaw preaches, drawing on Lamarck and against Darwin, is the doctrine of 'creative evolution', which he regards as a new Bible. The Preface to *Back to Methuselah* becomes, quite simply, a sacred text. According to Shaw, creative evolution is 'the genuinely scientific religion for which all wise men are now anxiously looking'.

We can easily understand what this new religion will offer in terms of life expectancy. It throws open the doors to a variable longevity, adapted to needs and desires. The average 70 years available to human beings today has been set for opportunistic reasons alone. There is nothing to stop humanity, if it wishes, raising the ceiling to 300 or 3,000 years, since 'among other matters apparently changeable at will is the duration of individual life'.

According to this logic death is also ultimately challenged. It cannot be considered as 'an eternal condition of life'; in reality it is merely 'an expedient introduced to provide for continual renewal without overcrowding'. The only remaining restriction is the number of people that can be supported by the Earth. If we were capable of enabling a larger number of generations to coexist, longevity would increase accordingly, until the time when the problem of overpopulation is entirely solved. At that point there would be nothing to stop human beings from becoming immortal.

After the Preface comes the play, when the theory is applied. Everything begins, as is only right, with Adam and Eve. They are created immortal but decide to accept death and to conceive children, thereby renouncing personal immortality in favour of the immortality of the species. The second episode takes place around 1920. The Barnabas brothers (one a biologist, the other a theologian) are writing a 'new gospel' in which they note that human life is short and announce that it will be extended to 300 years. In this way a man who today ends his days without really leaving behind the mental state of childhood, will have the time he needs to mature and develop his potential as he should. The means of effecting this biological revolution is disconcertingly simple. One need only believe in it and want it, but one must want it with all one's being. The following sequence unfolds 250 years later, in 2170. It is apparent that the revolution has taken place. The first examples of the new humanity, aged 270 or 280 (though they don't look it) are already drawing attention. One more jump in time and we are in the year 3000, on the shore of Galway Bay. The new human beings are living in the 'British Islands' and look contemptuously on the short-lived humanity living in the rest of the world (at that time it has not yet been decided whether they should be tolerated or exterminated). The last sequence takes place in the distant future, in 31920. Human beings have become theoretically immortal (they still die, but only by accident, having lived hundreds or thousands of years). The spirit has conquered the flesh and the organism's 'animal' functions have been reduced to the minimum. Women no longer bear children, who instead hatch in the adolescent state from eggs and have four years in which to indulge in the games of love, art and science (in a distant memory of humanity's former amusements). After this time they become adults and their lives completely spiritual, with almost no distinction between the sexes. The next step, apparently soon to be taken, is to abandon the bodily shell altogether for an existence conceived of as pure thought, free of the constraints of space and matter. This entire evolution is a simple matter of will, of human beings working on themselves.

It may have occurred to Shaw (still 'young' at 70, 80, 90) that he would be one of the elect destined to live 300 years and thereby heralding a new era for humanity

Shaw is known for his acerbic criticism of the society around him, and he was sometimes right on target. However, his sense of humour and perception of absurdity seem to have left him once he heard the siren song of utopia. This is the price paid by all utopians, all those who sing in praise of the radiant future. The song was indeed attractive, reflecting a current of opinion that, for two centuries, had been drawn to the idea of the radical transformation of the human condition. A new society would give rise to a new man, spiritually and biologically rejuvenated. It is here that the history of longevity meets that of communism.

In this light it is easy to understand why the Soviet experiment aroused Shaw's admiration, which he expressed in a non-conformist manner, but which remained admiration for all that.

Moreover it was not Marxism but Stalinism that so attracted him. The social determinism of the Marxist doctrine bothered Shaw quite as much as Darwinian biological determinism, and he rejected both Marx and Darwin. Communism, however, had followed the classic path between determinism and voluntarism. Stalinism was simply the transposition of Marxism into the terms of a boundless, irresistible voluntarism. Everything became possible, regardless of means and conditions, including the radical transformation of human nature. This pleased Shaw enormously. In 1949, a year before his death, he made one last effort of vituperation against genetic fatalism. No state could tolerate such a doctrine, he claimed, let alone a socialist state whose reason for existence was precisely to perfect society and the human being. So, the new Methuselahs would soon be born in the Soviet Union.

THE SOVIET REVOLUTION: *the battle against heredity*

Taking up the torch of the French Revolution, but with more ambitious aims and more powerful means, the Russian revolution made its goal to re-create the world and remould human beings. The new golden age would be characterized, in accordance with the archetype, by the rejuvenation of humanity and an explosion of the life force and intellectual power.[5]

The end of 'man's exploitation of man' would enable humanity to blossom. In order to reach this goal, the 'proletarian' ideology of communism advocated, in the first instance, the methodology of work (essentially of a manual nature): the work that – according to Engels's theory – had transformed monkeys into men would transform man into a 'new man'. The second grand principle, linked to work, was that of life in the community. For decades the education systems of the Soviet Union and other communist countries were based on the pedagogy of Makarenko, with its keywords 'work' and 'collectivity' (to which we should add 'brainwashing', a principle never openly advocated but widely used).

The 'new' man differed from the old not only in spirit but also in body. Trotsky, one of the leaders of the Russian revolution and of Soviet Russia, wrote an essay on this question in 1924, in which he says that human beings will become incomparably stronger, wiser and more subtle. They will learn to control physical processes such as breathing, the circulation of the blood, digestion and reproduction. But to achieve all this they must overcome the enemy of heredity, the tyrant that has been programming our lives for thousands and thousands of years in an unvarying and utterly unimaginative way. Like all the ills of the Ancien Régime, like the tsar and Capital, heredity will simply be abolished. If man wishes to transform himself into a superior social and biological being, he must start by abandoning biological fatalism. Trotsky ended his days as one of Stalin's victims; however, the conflict between the two men should not be allowed to obscure the fact that both express an unbridled voluntarism produced by the intoxication of a great revolution. If the Tsar had been defeated, why not human nature too?

Progress should be methodical, from the simple to the complex, starting with the plant world. The founding fathers of the new biology were Ivan Vladimirovich Michurin (1855–1935) and Trofim Denisovich Lysenko (1898–1976). The former had no training in biology; he was simply an amateur (and very imaginative) gardener. The latter was an agriculturalist who, with Stalin's support, became a kind of dictator of Soviet agriculture, promising superabundant harvests to the starving Russians. Between them these biological magicians managed to create a great profusion of new species of fruit trees and cereals, which seem to have been more mythical than real. They referred to Darwin as

Stalin referred to Marx, but were in fact far closer to Lamarck. Like Lamarck (and Bernard Shaw, who could at least plead that he had remained within the sphere of literature) they put their faith in the transmissibility of acquired characteristics. This allowed them to remould living organisms through a series of slight modifications. What was possible in plants should also be so in animals. Highly successful pigs and cows soon appeared, if not in the everyday world, then at least in Soviet mythology. Man should be next. Indeed he was already changing.

THE VIGOROUS OLD MEN OF THE CAUCASUS

It was at this time that the Caucasian centenarians made their remarkable entrance. Their dossier represents a rather mysterious chapter in the history of the quest for longevity and the debate around them ran for 50 years. The detractors of these fabulously old men spoke of biological impossibility; their supporters – including, aside from the Russians, some American scientists – accused the former of ignorance and jealousy. The controversy clearly took an ideological turn, with attitudes for and against depending largely on a person's view of the Soviet Union and the communist experiment.

How to Live to be 100, published in 1976 by the American anthropologist Sula Benet, is a typical example. Benet was much assisted by the Soviet authorities and has no trouble identifying a whole series of home-grown Methuselahs, whose secret lies in their great capacity for social integration, in striking contrast with American individualism.

It all began around 1930. Of course the regional traditions were certainly older; their strong ideological and media presence, however, dates from this time, which corresponds to the rise of Stalin in the political sphere and Lysenko in that of biology. One of the earliest accounts, dated 1930, is by the French communist writer Henri Barbusse who, in his book *Russie*, gives impressions from his trip to the land of the Soviets in 1927. An entire chapter is given over to his unforgettable meeting with the 'oldest man alive', enhanced with a few more general remarks on longevity.

The man in question was called Nicolas Chapkovsky and lived in a village in the Georgian province of Abkhazia. He was 146 years old. His physical condition was excellent, although he had given up swimming in the river, a sport he had practised for 120 years, preferably in winter. Very vigorous where sex was concerned, like all true centenarians, Chapkovsky was the father of a young woman of 26, whom he had conceived at the age of around 120.

A few years later, in 1937, a quick survey of a few villages around Sukhumi in Abkhazia identified no fewer than twelve people aged between 107 and 135. These old people, if such they can be called, were disconcertingly lively. The study states that 'several of them climbed the ladders themselves to pick the ripest bunches from the vines to give to the visitors'.

The youngest, a man of 107, was going through a difficult time: he was tormented by sexual longing and was looking for a young wife. To this end he cunningly declared his age as only 70, which was no problem given his appearance of glowing health. 'Unmasked by his contemporaries and those around him, he confessed, "I'm just about to get married; who wants to marry an old man of 100? But anyone would marry a man of 70."'

Even more impressive records were noted elsewhere in the same region, in particular those of a peasant farmer who had died at the age of 155 and another who was still alive at 150. Nor was such longevity to be found only in Abkhazia; all the valleys of the Caucasus produced similar figures. Near Groznyresearchers found two inhabitants, aged 147 and 166 respectively, who had known Chamyl, the great hero of the mid-nineteenth-century independence movement. These symbols of near-immortality among the Chechen people did not seem to bother the Russians of Stalin's day. The problem of nationalism had been resolved to everyone's satisfaction and the achievements of all ethnic groups were a reason for pride throughout the great Soviet family.

We see here an amalgam of two different motifs. The first is the natural longevity of the Caucasian peoples. These mountain-dwellers lived very long lives due to their natural surroundings and way of life: 'The mountains produce centenarians just as they produce great oak trees', explained Barbusse. Second, however, is the fact that these were not just any mountains; they were the Caucasus, Soviet mountains. The Caucasian centenarians proved the feasibility of a project dear to the heart of the regime. The circumstances from which they benefited were due not just to the Caucasian climate but also to the new social climate that had been established since the Revolution. The society deserved to have members who lived long lives. It was a society in which these still vigorous old people found their true role. Far from vegetating in peaceful fashion, they were noteworthy for their active participation in the life of their community, thus setting an example to the younger generation.

'In the USSR', wrote Dr Bogomoletz, 'it is possible not only to live from 100 to 150 years, but also to retain an honoured position as an active member of the socialist society'. Look at Comrade Kosoretz, member of a *kolkhoz* (collective farm), who, though more than 100 years old, continues to work as before, or Comrade Kusientzova who, aged 121, had no hesitation participating in the election of the Soviets.

The Caucasians were merely the avant-garde of the great army of centenarians who were already taking their place throughout all the regions of the Soviet Union, from Odessa to Vladivostok.

For decades the archipelago of centenarians played a role in obscuring that of the Gulag; the myth of longevity concealed the very real industry of death.

The pre-eminence of the Caucasians can also be explained – regardless of their real or imagined natural superiority to other groups – by another small but significant detail. Born in the small Georgian town of Gori, Stalin was himself a child of the Caucasus. The mythical amplification of Caucasian vitality was an element in the chorus of flattery that was unceasingly addressed to the master of the Kremlin. In spite of this, Stalin had the good taste to die at the age of 74. We do not like to think what the effects might have been had his life extended into the third millennium.

THE BOGOMOLETZ SERUM AND THE REJUVENATING EFFECTS
OF THE RADIANT FUTURE

Dr Aleksandr Bogomoletz was born in 1881 and began his career as a member of the Institut Pasteur in Paris. After the Russian revolution he became engaged in activities that linked medicine and politics in a unique revolutionary movement. President of the Ukrainian Academy of Science, founder of the Kiev Institute of Biology and Experimental Pathology, winner of the Stalin Prize and member of the Supreme Soviet of the USSR, he is recognizably the kind of transformist scientist or scientific activist who, with Stalin's support, enjoyed considerable power in Soviet society. He became the great communist expert on longevity, publishing *The Prolongation of Life* in 1938.

This work offers a full review of Soviet centenarians, not only from the Caucasus but from all the other regions in the USSR as well. There are tens of thousands of them, not far off Lejoncourt's old statistics, although this time it was no longer possible to accuse some boyar of exaggeration. The race was multiplying in a clear and encouraging way.

This was only natural, since human beings were destined to live 150 years or even more in good health. To arrive at this total Bogomoletz, like so many of his predecessors, adopts Buffon's method. He multiplies 20 or 25 by 7, giving a good average of a century and a half. In any case, '100 years is not a maximum for human life'; this is an obvious fact, as proved by the profusion of centenarians.

The problem remains of understanding why human beings only rarely reach such an age. The causes of this, the doctor explains, are primarily social in nature. How can one possibly live 150 years in a capitalist society? Exploitation, hunger, cold and overwork prevent the majority of the population from enjoying their entire capital of longevity. In addition there are reasons of a biological order, all the afflictions and maladies that undermine the human organism.

The causes lead us directly to their solutions. The first step is to abolish exploitation and establish social equality and the respect for work. This is exactly what has been done in the Soviet Union and the result, as has been observed, has been a rise in the number of centenarians. The obvious conclusion is that, 'It is only in the conditions of socialism that the social surroundings can be favourable to the health and longevity of man'.

Next it is necessary to combat disease and strengthen the organism. This is not as complex as it seems, since Dr Bogomoletz has perfected the necessary means. His main discovery is the cytotoxic serum that bears his name, the famous 'Bogomoletz serum'. When injected into the conjunctive tissue it stimulates activity here, failure of which is responsible for a major part of biological malfunctioning. This is an almost universal remedy. The preface to the French edition of 1950, by Professor Henri

Desoille of the Faculty of Medicine in Paris, provides an impressive inventory of its effects. The serum acts, with equal success, in the treatment of infections, cancer, fractures and some forms of mental illness. In addition, and above all, it preserves longevity. This type of treatment can be combined with blood transfusions that also have the power, according to Dr Bogomoletz, to heal a wide range of afflictions, such as cancer and blindness.

Social and physical health are the keys to 150 years (or more) of life. Everything was developing perfectly, except for the health of Dr Bogomoletz. He died in 1946, in full creative flight, at the age of 65 – a bit of a blow for a longevity expert.

Fortunately the battle against death was being fought on several fronts. Among the solutions suggested, that of the biologist Nikolai P. Krenke (1892–1939), who also died young, shows undeniable originality. According to his theory, opposing tendencies of ageing and rejuvenation are at war in each organism. Instead of a linear movement towards death there is a more complex movement through 'age cycles'. Krenke had been working on plants, but there was no reason not to extend the method, which proved that old age was not fatal; it could be followed by a period of rejuvenation, a new youth.

A small masterpiece on this theme was written by Traian Savulescu, professor of agronomy and President of the Romanian Academy. Here is what he said to his scientific colleagues in 1952:

> The pace of the processes of ageing and rejuvenation depends to a large extent on external conditions. For animals and plants it depends on the surrounding physical environment, for men also on the social environment.
>
> In capitalist society the cycle of rejuvenation is brutally interrupted. Old age implacably follows its rectilinear, descending course. Children and young people age early,

serious social ills, economic crises and wars decimate the population [. . .] These are the signs of ageing, which ends, inevitably and before time, in death.

In socialist society the social factors, the economic base, the relations of production and the superstructure inhibit ageing and accelerate the return of the cycle of rejuvenation.

There could be no finer exposition of the close relationship that binds the rejuvenation of the world to that of the human being, revolution to longevity.

Stalinism had set up a complete mythology that overlaid every aspect of real history and ordinary life. Although cracked and losing credibility, this fictitious discourse on the world, supported by the transformist project inherent in Stalinism, survived the Red dictator's death. Its ebb was slow and affected the core ideology only very partially.

Longevity followed the same pattern. The Caucasians became thinner on the ground, but did not disappear altogether. The year 1974 saw celebrations for the 140th birthday of a lady in that region, who died the following year. Her life story, which is most edifying, was reconstructed in great detail by Sula Benet in the work mentioned above. She was 85 when she joined a collective farm; at 104 she travelled to Moscow for the USSR's first agricultural exhibition; at 128 she was still working. Her speed and skill made her a model for the other workers.

In his book promisingly entitled *À quoi rêvent les savants soviétiques* ('What the Soviet Scientists Dream of') and published in 1958, the French scientific journalist Lucien Barnier included rejuvenation among the dreams in question. By means of injections of novocaine, the Soviets were giving elderly people back not only their hair colour – in itself a small thing – but also, and above all, 'the hope of a long life' with 'memory and the ability to work'.

Around 1960 the aim remained unchanged: 150 years of life without illness. This was revised down over the following years, but still remained fairly ambitious: at least a century for children born in the year 2000. The radiant future was losing some of its brilliance, but continued to offer the best of all possible worlds.

DEATH IN CHECKMATE

At the same time the secret mechanism of death was being explored in the hope that its workings could be revealed, enabling it to be controlled, avoided or made to run backwards. If the process did prove reversible this would open up wonderful prospects for the new man.

The resurrection of the dead was a preoccupation of Soviet medicine. Just after the war it was learnt that one group of scientists had developed a method described (with good reason) as 'complex', in which blood was pumped into the arteries of the 'almost deceased' patient, who was simultaneously given artificial respiration. The war provided abundant raw materials for experiments of this kind. One of the Soviet soldiers to be brought back to life was Igor, a sergeant 'killed' by an exploding mine just as his battalion was entering Berlin. The complex method was applied and, twenty minutes or so after his clinical death, Igor opened his eyes and asked for water. The next day his first reaction was, of course, to ask whether the Red Army had taken Berlin.

A decade or so later Lucien Barnier, an expert in Soviet marvels, rightly presented resurrection as a complementary method to rejuvenation. The phenomenon seemed already to have been mastered: 'Soviet scientists have resuscitated dogs an hour after their theoretical death, monkeys twenty minutes after and men five or six minutes after'.

Popularizations of medical advances, closer in practice to political propaganda than to science, presented death as a 'curable' ill that would one day be treated effectively. The strongest assertions in this regard came from the British physician John D. Bernal, a communist scientist who kept abreast with the research of his Soviet colleagues. In the February 1952 issue of the international journal *Défense de la paix* he published an astounding article entitled 'La science peut faire reculer la mort' ('Science can push back death'):

Treating illnesses is in itself an admission of defeat; a truly healthy society should not allow illness to appear within it. Neither old age nor illness are necessary ills [. . .] Death itself is not an absolute necessity, but one determined by circumstance; when we understand more we shall be able to delay it and perhaps to eliminate it.

This will happen in the not-too-distant future, 'in countries where men use their intelligence to create well-being for all, a new spirit, a new culture' – in other words in the Soviet Union and China.

The elimination of death: here is a decisive step that Condorcet had not dared to take. He had even been careful to make clear that 'man will not become immortal'. Even science fiction had rarely gone so far. Yet a physician intoxicated by the new order could do so (as George Bernard Shaw had done before him). Bernal was speaking in the name of a revolution that represented a step up to a stage above all that humanity had achieved or dreamed of throughout its history.

Illness was a bourgeois 'privilege', and perhaps death as well; both were biological projections of the failures of the social organism. A sick society will produce sick individuals, a healthy society will produce healthy individuals and a political system proclaiming its immortality might perhaps produce immortal individuals. The quest for longevity had always flirted with ideology; this time it had allowed itself to be quite simply possessed.

Battle against Time, a science fiction story by Valentina Zhuravlyova published in 1958, provides a perfect example of the communist logic of immortality. The vital functions of a doctor with an incurable disease are suspended (by extreme cold) for nineteen years. In the meantime – if still rather quickly – communism triumphs and, quite logically, there are no more sick people. The time has come to revive the dying man, who is amazed that his own doctor seems not to have aged at all in the intervening years. The explanation is simple:

We have conquered old age. It was thought to be an irreversible process. We have proved that, on the contrary, the process is reversible. For the moment this is only true within certain conditions; with time we shall completely overcome it. But this is not the only miracle. When you leave hospital, you won't recognize anybody. That's communism!

Today this may make us amused, or indignant; but above all we must try to understand it. This triumph of longevity explains the seduction of communism better than any argument, and particularly its most hard-line manifestations, such as Stalinism and Maoism. Human beings have always dreamed of a different world and a better human condition, freed from ancestral servitude. The new society seemed capable of turning this dream into reality and projecting humanity forward into a world where everything would be different. It was time to remove the word impossible from the language, including the language of science.

This hope, which had been around a long time and seemed on the verge of becoming reality, explains the strength and persistence of the illusion, despite the denials of history. Nothing is more painful that the demythologization of a fairy tale. Nothing hurts more than renouncing a utopia. Let us be indulgent towards George Bernard Shaw; like everyone else he needed something to believe in.

To the poor mortals of the West (at least the more naïve among them) the East appeared as an inexhaustible fountain of youth. Bucharest came to rival Moscow. A stay at Dr Ana Aslan's 'centenarian factory' in the Romanian capital, reinforced with a course of 'gerovital' (a medicine based on procaine), was apparently the best way to regain one's health and, possibly, youth.

Unfortunately the statistics told a different story. Life expectancy in the communist countries was at a standstill or indeed falling, whereas it was rising in the West. The reasons for this are easy to identify: poor working conditions, poor nutrition, inadequate health systems, and so on. Today there is a difference of almost ten years between the ex-communist world and the West (in the latter's favour evidently). The fabled Caucasians have disappeared, probably dying of old age. Anyone hoping for a long life should move to a Western metropolis rather than the Caucasus mountains (let alone Moscow or Bucharest).

EIGHTEEN HUMAN SPECIES AND 2 BILLION YEARS:
the future according to Stapledon

Throughout the last two centuries space and time have continually expanded. As long as the Earth had not been fully explored, it was the space of our planet that stimulated the imagination. In the nineteenth century the solar system began to make an impact; fabulous peoples whose homes had formerly been located at the ends of the Earth or on distant islands were now moved out to the planets (chiefly Venus and Mars). These days we have taken a further great step; it is our pleasure – in our imaginations for the moment – to travel the galaxies.

According to the Bible, Earth and humanity have existed for only a few millennia (since 4004 BC according to James Usher, a calculation that held until the nineteenth century), while the end may be far closer. In the eighteenth century Buffon suggested that the Earth was 75,000 years old, that it had supported life for the last 40,000 and that all life would be extinguished in 168,000 years time. In the mid-nineteenth century the British geologist Charles Lyell was already estimating the age of our planet as 240 million years. Today the figure has risen to almost 5 billion years. Man has also got older. When the nineteenth century discovered prehistory the age of humanity was initially set at around 100,000 years, then at hundreds of thousands of years and finally at more than a million or several million years. The future expanded symmetrically. Flammarion believed life had existed for 10 million years and, man included, had another 10 million to go. H. G. Wells's time-traveller witnesses the end of life on earth in 30 million years time. Today the Earth's future is estimated as at least 5 billion years (as long as its past); theoretically humanity may have the same period ahead, unless it degenerates or perishes in some cataclysm.

Space and time no longer provided a fixed backdrop. They had been fertilized by two powerful ideas of the nineteenth and twentieth centuries: evolution (in the biological sense) and progress (in the technological, social and moral sense), as well as by their opposite, the idea of degeneration or decadence. So the human species was subject to continual change by natural factors and also, beyond a certain threshold, by the presumed capacity of man to modify his own nature. Wells imagines the man of the year

1,000,000 as shaped like an octopus, with a large head (development of the brain), a body reduced to the minimum (reduction of animal functions) and a bunch of tentacles. Another scenario, which Wells sets in the year 802701, shows humanity splitting into two different (and equally degenerate) species. Both cases were strict results of the forces of evolution; however the idea spread (as we have seen with Shaw and the communist experience) that, instead of following this long path and bowing to the arbitrary decisions of nature, man should act according to his own plan and transform himself.

All these currents come together in *Last and First Men* (1930), a work by the British writer Olaf Stapledon (1886–1950). This long text is clearly a work of fiction, yet the view of the future is that of a historian or philosopher. The expansion of time, the refinement of evolutionist theory and the oscillation (so typical of the time) between determinism and voluntarism, progress and decadence, are given remarkable expression in this work. For Wells a million years was a lot. Stapledon proposes to relate human history for the next two billion years. For Wells evolution led to one or two human species; Stapledon describes no fewer than eighteen species (with, in addition, a multitude of subspecies and transitional variants). In Wells's work the evolutionary path runs straight ahead. Stapledon imagines countless paths leading in all directions, intersecting, going up and down, endlessly creating and re-creating men, supermen and submen. It is a cyclical history whose overall direction remains upward. Lastly Wells is still depicting a phase in which nature rules and its action is slow. For Stapledon evolution is determined in equal measure by biological and environmental factors and by the conscious, purposefully directed action of man. The ideas Wells expresses were revolutionary in the late nineteenth century. Although barely 30 years separate his pioneering novels from Stapledon's work, the change in the way of seeing things is astonishing. True, all this is just literature: it is in literature, however, that dreams and projects are expressed in their state of ideal purity; then science comes along and does its best.

In 10 million years time the Earth will belong to our direct descendant, the 'second man'. He looks like us, but better: he is taller, with a larger skull and an estimated life expectancy of 200 years. As a projection of longevity this is, it must be said, a little disappointing. Haller and Hufeland promised us the same span just around the corner. Still, better late than never – at least we get an opportunity for direct observation of the new distribution of the ages of life, spread across two centuries. The 'second man' reaches puberty at 20, maturity at about 50, while around 190 his powers begin to weaken and he generally dies fairly soon after, before experiencing true old age.

The men of the third species, by contrast, have a comparatively short life of only 60 years. This regression in terms of longevity is compensated by other qualities and accomplishments. It is these men who, through biological manipulation, invent a semi-artificial species, the fourth man. This is in fact no more than a truly enormous brain, encased in a concrete shell (his 'skull') and kept alive by a collection of tubes, electric circuits and various other mechanisms. Being pure brain he has a powerful intelligence and infinite curiosity, but lacks all feelings and moral scruples. He becomes master of the planet, reducing the previous species – his creators – to slavery. Theoretically he is immortal. This fourth species multiplies until there are 10,000 individuals, each encased in a shell and communicating telepathically.

Aware of both his power and his weakness (the lack of a body and all human qualities dependent on it), the fourth man in turn makes the fifth man, attempting to produce a more balanced result. His creation then exterminates him. The fifth man is like a more perfect version of the second (and also, more or less, of ourselves); he is immensely tall (twice our height) with a large brain (but in normal proportion with the human body). Initially his life expectancy is 3,000 years, but this is later extended, following successive refinements, to 50,000 years. It is this man who leaves the Earth, which is threatened with collision with the Moon, and moves to Venus.

The 'Venusian' history of man lasts a little longer than his earthly phase. One of the later species migrates to Neptune, which sees the flowering of the eighteenth (and last) human species, the most remarkable of all in terms of its physical, intellectual and emotional capacities. It is also notably long-lived, enjoying the near-immortality of 250,000 years. True immortality is, however, never attained. Paradoxically these men, whose lives extend over tens or hundreds of thousands of years, are even more troubled by the awareness of death than our own ephemeral species. To die on the threshold of immortality seems a far graver injustice than our everyday 'familiar' death, which is always with us today from the moment of our birth. Yet it is precisely death that gives meaning to life.

The last man's end is unexpected and unfair. A cosmic explosion produces radiation that permanently affects the sun, planets and life itself. Everything comes to an end, stoically accepted by these superior humans.

After depicting innovations of every kind, Stapledon denies the last man what had by then become quite a commonplace escape route in the form of migration beyond the solar system, to other parts of the galaxy or different galaxies. On this point he kept to the nineteenth-century framework: man is still held within the confines of our planetary world.

In 1958 Professor Jameson perfected the technology that was to enable his body to remain intact indefinitely after his death. This involved encasing it in a small space vessel to be sent into orbit around the Earth, where the void of space would protect the flesh from any form of corruption. His desire was put into practice and for 40 million years the professor fulfilled his posthumous destiny as a 'satellite'. In the meantime humanity disappeared and the Earth became deserted. The satellite was eventually discovered by an interstellar expedition by the Zoromes, a species living on the planet Zor, located millions of light years from our solar system. The Zoromes have long ago abandoned their bodies, retaining only the brain, which is contained in a metal case and provided for by means of artificial extensions (including four legs, six arms and several eyes). They communicate telepathically. Ultimately they are immortal. Found by these curious creatures, Professor Jameson's brain is brought back to life and placed inside one of their machines. Thus the professor (or rather his brain) begins a new life as an immortal.

The above is a summary of *The Jameson Satellite* by the American writer Neil R. Jones, published in 1931 (to be followed by twenty or more further episodes, the last published in 1951).[6] We are a long way here from the quality of Wells's writing or the dialectical rigour of Stapledon's argument. Nevertheless, the 'Jameson dossier' occupies an interesting place in the imaginary manifestation of longevity, since it represents a synthesis of several trends and gave rise to later developments in its turn.

In the first place, it deals with the project of preserving the body in a state of apparent death in order to revive it in a more or less distant future. In 1766 the British anatomist and surgeon John Hunter (1728–1793) had carried out an experiment in which he froze several live carp and then defrosted them, hoping to find them still alive. Unfortunately the poor carp did not survive the treatment. Hunter was very disappointed:

> Till this time I had imagined that it might be possible to prolong life to any period by freezing a person in the frigid zone, as I thought all action and waste would cease until the body was thawed. I thought that if a man would give up the last ten years of his life to this kind of alternate oblivion and action, it might be prolonged to one thousand years: and by getting himself thawed every hundred years, he might learn what had happened during his frozen condition.[7]

This 'experiment' was repeated in 1890 by the French writer Louis Boussenard who, in his short novel *10,000 ans dans un bloc de glace* ('10,000 Years in a Block of Ice'), describes the revival of an arctic explorer who was enclosed in ice in 1886; 10,000 years later, in 11886, he is discovered by the heirs of today's human beings, who have meanwhile greatly evolved (faster than in Wells's work) into 'big heads', supported by feeble bodies and having the gift of levitation. Clearly (as in Jameson's story), this was a case of fortuitous survival. For another instance of this idea see Zhuravlyova's story (quoted above and published after Jones's) in which the powers of cold to preserve the body are used deliberately for therapeutic purposes.

Secondly, *The Jameson Satellite* clearly displays a degree of 'positive discrimination' in favour of the brain over the rest of the body, reflecting a trend illustrated by several authors. We have seen how, each in his own way, Wells, Stapledon and Shaw regarded the development of the brain (in other words of pure thought and consciousness) and the corresponding fading of the 'animal' functions as a probable consequence of evolution. It

Resurrected after 10,000 years in a block of ice, to discover an entirely altered human species: an illustration from Louis Boussenard, *10,000 ans dans un bloc de glace* (Paris, 1890).

was only the brain that truly deserved to become immortal. Sex and food were all right as amusements in the context of an ordinary lifetime, but for eternity intelligence was enough (this way of seeing things was a secular continuation of the spiritualized hereafter of the religions). Auguste Comte had expressed an interesting idea in a similar vein, reflecting his ideal of asceticism and spiritualization: he believed that the brain would be capable of 'wearing out two bodies and perhaps three'[8] (this was at a time when most people died at a less advanced age than today and could comfort themselves with the illusion that the brain remained forever young, even in a worn-out body; today the opposite model seems more current: the body lasts while, more and more often, the brain gives way). The Belgian writer Marcel Thiry came up with an unexpected solution in his story *Le Concerto pour Anne Queur* (1949), in which he describes a method of reviving the dead that preserves only their brains and skeletons. According to him this results in human beings of rather unpleasant appearance, but wise, just and spiritual to the highest degree.

One last point illustrated by Professor Jameson's adventures is the removal of barriers blocking access to space (at a time when Stapledon was forbidding his last man to overstep the boundaries of the solar system). Thus spatial and temporal infinity go hand in hand. Immortality would be unbearable within an enclosed space and is workable only when man is given the capacity for infinite travel in an endless adventure of consciousness.

The fictional character of Jameson was to have very real heirs. I shall return to this later.

TWO OPPONENTS OF METHUSELAH: *Karel Čapek and Aldous Huxley*

Yet – as always – there are those who want none of it. Are these people opponents of progress or simply proponents of common sense?

One year after Shaw, and apparently responding to him, the Czech writer Karel Čapek (1890–1938) placed longevity centre stage in his play *Věc Makropulos* ('The Makropoulos Secret', 1922). Čapek's heroine is a young woman of 337. Born in 1585, she has enjoyed the benefits of a prescription for long life orig- inally devised by her father, Dr Makropoulos, for Emperor Rudolph II. As the treatment needs to be repeated after a period of 300 years, the 'old young woman' has to decide whether or not to renew it. People around her find out about her father's document and a long debate follows. The generous response would be to allow all of humanity to benefit. A more elitist approach is also suggested: the recipe should be the preserve of a small group (an 'aristocracy of longevity'), thus ensuring that they would rule over the others. However, although initially very excited, the protagonists gradually become aware of the risks of an excessively prolonged life. The doctor's daughter describes her incurable boredom. She is certainly afraid of death, yet she envies mortals their ordinary fate. Feelings, passions and all that give meaning to human life have their place within a normal span, in a life both haunted and given value by death. Nothing of life's tumults remains in an existence lasting several hundred years; nothing has value for someone who sails undisturbed down the river of time, and such indifference is worse than death. The paradoxical conclusion is that without death life is unliveable. The decision is taken to burn the 'Makropoulos recipe', that bearer of false hope. The only wise option is to accept life as it is.

In British literature every century has been marked by an 'anti-longevity' expert. The eighteenth century had Swift, the nineteenth Besant and in the twentieth century the torch was taken up by Aldous Huxley, who dissects the myth of longevity in his novel *After Many a Summer Dies the Swan*, published in 1939. The story's protagonists are the American multimillionaire Stoyte, who wants to prolong his life, and Dr Obispo, who is preparing to treat him with an extract of the intestinal flora of carp, a fish known for its long life. This revolutionary method has already been used by an English earl, who treated both his housekeeper and himself in the late eighteenth century, devouring raw fish intestines for decades. The result was magnificent: at the age of 81 the rejuvenated old man successfully fathered three illegitimate children.

A family scandal ensued, obliging him to hide away in the cellar of his house, where he was found by our Americans. They are able to observe the medicine's incontrovertible success: at more than 200 the count is in the pink, as is his lady-friend, the ex-house-keeper, and the pair of them seem to be having a lot of fun, in a rather noisy and brutish way. Something, however, seems not quite right and soon all becomes clear: they have both lost their reason and descended the biological ladder to the level of the monkeys.

It would seem that, though the human machine may survive, the mind does not follow. Longevity must be paid for by intellectual regression. This is a serious dilemma for our multimillionaire: he has to choose between death in the short term and the carefree life of a human monkey. Our would-be immortal finds the strength to put forward one last, timid argument in favour of the second solution: 'They seem to keep themselves entertained. In their own way of course!'

We can observe that neither Huxley nor Čapek denies the validity of the biological project in itself. They accept the possibility of a lifetime extended across several centuries. But what would such a life be like? Would it really be worth living? For these two writers, in different ways, extreme longevity simply leads to dehumanization. For Shaw, conversely, it was the only way for humanity to realize its potential. Here we have two divergent approaches to our subject, two opposing views of human destiny.

7 The Religion of Health

The Late Twentieth Century and Beyond

DEATH DEMOTED

Today everything is changing very fast indeed. The West is currently inventing a system of civilization that is entirely new in comparison to every other cultural synthesis seen in history.[1] Life expectancy in its turn has lengthened in spectacular fashion. Our ideas of longevity and our corresponding projects have changed accordingly.

Around 1900 life expectancy in the West was a little over 45 years; by 1950 it had increased to 66; in most Western countries today it is between 76 and 79. We have gained over 30 years in the space of a century. This advance is due mainly to the reduction in infant mortality (still very high around 1900, even among the more privileged classes); it also reflects, however, a real increase in length of life: more people are living to an advanced age. Statistically speaking, we are further now from 1900 than 1900 was from Greco-Roman antiquity.

For thousands of years people had been 'familiarized' with death, which was very much a part of family life, routinely claiming children and young people as recently as the early twentieth century. Today this phenomenon has all but disappeared. Death has become less present and, as a result, we have got out of the habit of dying. Once familiar, death has now become a stranger to us. In this respect the twentieth century marked a turning-point in human history (a revolution due even more to improved hygiene than to medical advance. From this point of view running water is one of the greatest accomplishments in history, as important as the most famous scientific discoveries.)

Two further elements must be taken into consideration. The first is an ever more apparent longevity among women; in the developed countries the gap between the life expectancies of men and women is now some six to eight years in favour of the latter (80 or 82 years as opposed to 73 or 74). Justice at last! Despite being traditionally regarded as less capable of long life than men, women (partially liberated from their former enslavement to biology) have demonstrated their incontestable superiority (in terms of both averages and overall records). Secondly, for both men and women, old age now starts later. This is a reflection of both biology and mentalities. In the nineteenth century the average age of menopause for women was around 45; now it is usually well over 50. Today's man or woman of 70 is in a similar position to that of a 50-year-old in the nineteenth century. Not only are they in far better health than those of a corresponding age in times gone by, they also act in a more 'youthful' way and are no longer seen as old by other people.

Death has been demoted, both in actual fact and still more in our minds, having apparently lost all positive connotations. This is entirely new. Preceding generations always tried to find some balance between the values of life and the meaning of death. For religions, and particularly for Christians, death was simply a new beginning, a door open to the Absolute. Ultimately it could even appear as a kind of deliverance. This 'salutary' aspect of death is disappearing from today's attitudes. Even among believers there now seem very few who would sacrifice their earthly life for an uncertain hereafter. Life has become almost completely secularized, putting both the hereafter and, implicitly, death itself in an uncomfortable position.

Religion aside, historically there were other ways of ascribing value to death and, in particular, of using it to give a higher meaning to life. Goethe's hero Young Werther expressed the intensity of his love by killing himself. This 'literary' suicide ushered in the world of Romanticism, with its real suicides. In the choice between honour and life the rule that was proclaimed, if not necessarily upheld, always favoured honour (kill the enemy or kill oneself); and there was nothing more noble than to shed one's blood for a great cause, particularly for one's country. All in all, as Seneca said, perhaps more important than life itself was the manner of leaving it. Death set the definitive seal on the quality of a person's biography.

These spiritual, heroic times seem now to be over. Today's 'Westerners' just do not want to die any more. No ideology, not even the nationalism that has been responsible for so much carnage, now provides a sufficiently convincing reason to sacrifice one's life. War itself has become a matter for professionals. Conversely, the only ideology that does have a powerful presence is that of health, whether it be the health of the immediate environment, of the planet, or individual health (the fight against disease, prolonging life and youth). The hysteria around 'mad cow disease' is symptomatic. Nothing rouses public opinion more than the fear of sickness and death. The new frontier of the twenty-first century will be that of biology and ecology. Together they are already almost a new kind of religion.

TALES OF IMMORTALITY

A glance at literature is also instructive here.[2] We have already noted that longevity as a literary theme usually goes hand in hand with the complementary theme of death, seen as a necessary way out. In her story *The Mortal Immortal* (published in 1833), Mary Shelley relates the tragedy of a man condemned to eternal life who, at the age of 323 (still young for an immortal), stares with terror into the eternity he faces. Death must come; it may be put off as long as possible (the legitimate desire for longevity), yet nevertheless come it must. Otherwise life becomes unbearable and, worse still, loses all meaning. Illustration of this is provided by *El Inmortal* ('The Immortal', 1949), a story by Jorge Luis Borges, in which the reader is surprised to discover immortality among the most primitive of human beings, the African Troglodytes, mentioned by the authors of antiquity. These people live in holes in the ground and feed on snakes; such is the paradoxical yet logical result of an eternity leading nowhere at all. The Troglodytes have withdrawn into themselves, abandoning all contact with the world and even with each other. Nothing is important to them, everything is the same. In these conditions, it would be better to die. Homer, who himself became immortal after drinking from a river that flowed through the land of the Troglodytes, spent long centuries searching for the 'opposite' river, whose water would give him back the right to die (and, fortunately for him, eventually found it).

It seems to me that there has been a certain evolution on this point. The literature on immortality written in the last few decades remains clearly split into those for and those against, but the fors are making progress. Immortality pure and simple has been advanced as a solution that might not necessarily be bad, in fact quite the opposite. Roger Zelazny, one of the most influential American science-fiction writers, gives his verdict in the novel *This Immortal*, published in 1966. His hero (provisionally called Conrad) passes through the centuries, periodically changing his name and identity in order to go unnoticed among mortals. Apparently he does not get bored. His interminable life is always different, like a montage of many lives. So it seems the secret is to conceive of immortality in terms of perpetual creativity, providing a continual motivation for existence.

174

The Immortals (1968) by James Gunn offers a glimpse of how immortality might be feasible (a young man has a kind of immunity to death, which is then passed on by transfusion to other characters). The plot of this series of adventures does not show immortality as either good or bad in itself; it all depends on how you intend to use it.

We should also note the end of Jack Vance's novel *To Live Forever* (1956), which suggests that immortality would be a precious gift for human beings capable of 'taking possession' of infinite space and finding an infinite variety of new experiences:

> Only in the infinity of the universe can the immortal reach a state of development consonant with his or her immortal nature. The planet-bound, the socially constrained, are mortal; to organize and strive together is their natural lot. The immortal can never be limited to social convention, to the surface of only one whirling sphere. Planets, cities, societies – they are fetters; an immortal so constrained will become, finally, dulled and meagre [   ] The vast freedom of years that immortality imparts must be matched by a corresponding freedom of experience; only the limitless frontier of space is the proper condition for eternal life.[3]

Of course we are dealing with literary fiction here. No project with any claims to scientific validity would promise immortality today, or indeed the conquest of the stars. Yet Vance's logic can function effectively on a more modest scale. Three hundred years of life, for example, was probably too long a period of time in traditional societies, where things changed very little, if at all, and people were condemned to live in the same environment according to the same rules. But today, or tomorrow, why not? In a world of permanent transformation a very long life would become truly fascinating; it would consist of experiences that were always new in an environment that was never the same.

But what life expectancy is it reasonable to envisage? Has the ceiling really moved? Or has there rather been a kind of 'democratization' of 'great age', with an increasing number of people reaching 70, 80 or 90, but no real movement in the upper limit? People lived to be 100 in antiquity, too, but they were extremely rare. Today there are many more. This is clearly an advance, but it is not necessarily a biological revolution.

The most recent records for longevity belong to a Japanese man, Shigechiyo Izumi, who died in 1986 aged 120 years and 8 months, and the absolute record-holder Jeanne Calment, a French woman who died on 4 August 1997, aged 122 years, 5 months and 11 days. These are modest totals in comparison to St Mungo's 185 years, Thomas Parr's 152 or the longevity of the famous old men of the Caucasus, still hale and hearty at 150. The difference is that Jeanne Calment had a valid birth certificate; the same cannot be said for the other records, all of which rest entirely on 'oral tradition' and the all-too human tendency to believe in miracles.

It seems reasonable then to conclude that up until now no one has lived longer than 122 years. Is this an absolute limit, or is it relative and provisional? There are two opposing views. Some experts believe in an unbreakable barrier (at least as long as human beings remain as they are). Around ten years ago this was set at about 115, or 120 years at the most. However, it was broken – not by much, but broken all the same – by Jeanne Calment. There is already talk of a more generous range, perhaps from 113 to 124.

Yet supposing there were to be no limit at all, or that the limit were gradually pushed back? In his book *Maximum Life Span*

Jeanne Calment,
champion of
longevity.

(1983), Ray Walford, professor of pathology at the University of
California, Los Angeles, puts forward the idea of an 'extensible'
life expectancy: 120 years today, maybe even 150, ultimately rising
to 300 years. In France (where the 'Jeanne Calment effect' has
stimulated optimism), Gabriel Simonoff, professor of nuclear
physics at the University of Bordeaux, also states – in his book *La
Nouvelle éternité* ('The New Eternity', 1993) – that the immediate
goal would be to live 120 years 'in perfect health and in full possession of our faculties'. However, he suggests that, in the near
future, this figure will rise to 600 years, as demonstrated, he
believes, by all scientific projections (when accidents and other
circumstances are included, actual life expectancy would be
around 350 years). It goes without saying that this would involve
a new distribution of the stages of life. No one imagines living
several centuries in a state of advanced decrepitude.

The goal is very clear; the difficult part is how to attain it. How should we proceed in order to live a long life, extending not only our time but also our youth? I shall begin with the simplest, cheapest and most commonly employed method, that of pretence.

In reality it is possible to 'lengthen' life, even if its ultimate limit is not really extended, by redistributing time within the period we have at our disposal. Instead of living only one life, we can live several, living each successive stage in a different way and giving each an ever more pronounced degree of autonomy.

Stage one: childhood. Philippe Ariès has observed that, before the eighteenth century, children 'did not exist'. They were seen as incomplete beings, no more than potential adults. Then families began to invest more in their offspring, first the upper classes, then the lower. Nevertheless, children remained miniature adults into the early twentieth century. If we look at the images of the period we see little people dressed and adorned just like their parents. With the passing years they had to learn the same long, tiring lesson, enabling them to behave as responsible adults. Although childhood was valued in the eighteenth and nineteenth centuries, its value lay not in itself but in its role as preparation for the future.[4]

This attitude underwent a very rapid change during the twentieth century, and particularly in recent decades. The intrinsic values of childhood are now better recognized and guaranteed. Childhood has become a truly distinct stage of life. But there is something else too: between childhood proper and maturity another stage has appeared, hitherto practically unknown; this is adolescence. Although differently delineated from one society to the next, or from one interpretation to the next, adolescence is now asserting its own values ever more clearly in territory won from both child-hood and adulthood. Indeed not only does it assert them, it very frequently imposes them on the other stages of life. Today it seems that mimicking adolescence is the surest method of regaining youth, much more certain than Dr Voronoff's implant or time spent in Dr Aslan's establishment. The current has been reversed. In the old days young people used to imitate adults; today it is the adults who are trying to stay up-to-date by learning from those younger than themselves. We can see this everywhere, from fashion to the way people behave. Every generation has apparently been rejuvenated through an 'infusion of adolescence', at least if we do not look beneath the surface.

Every day in the street we can admire fit, healthy adults roller-skating by, while the elderly travel slightly more sedately on scooters. Not so long ago roller-skates were the preserve of adolescents and scooters of children. Today's children prefer to spend their time staring at their computer screens, leaving the playthings of childhood to their grandparents. The implacable logic of the stages of life has at last become a thing of the past.

With childhood, then adolescence, followed by an extended period of maturity also bearing the hallmarks of youth, life is getting longer, offering both a greater number of stages and the retention of youthful energy.

Yet the most remarkable accomplishment of this strategy is the transformation of what we used to call old age into what is now known as the 'third age'.

Before considering the representation of the third age, we should note that the issues this involves arise out of developments in the real world. The increase in life expectancy, not to say longevity, has resulted in a phenomenon unprecedented in history: the massive presence of elderly people in the Western societies of today and their highly significant and ever growing importance in the overall structure of the population. While extreme longevity may be advancing more slowly, 'normal longevity' – 65, 70, 80 years plus – has become entirely commonplace. This suggests the rather disturbing vision of a retired population that, in the not-so-distant future, runs the risk of becoming almost as large as the active population that supports it.

Numbers aside, the second significant change relates to the physical condition of people in this category, which shows a clear improvement in most cases, thanks to advances in medicine and hygiene and modern technological aids (domestic gadgets, means of transport). As a result one can, theoretically, lead a normal, active life to a fairly advanced age.

Once again, it is not the individual cases, found in all periods, that make the difference, but the fact that this has become a mass phenomenon.

One more step and reality meets mythology: it is not enough for old age to be improved, it is becoming quite simply a new youth. When people retire they enter a quite distinct phase of life. This is no longer seen, mythologically speaking, as a gradually declining continuation of the preceding stage; rather it is a new beginning that, in addition to the knowledge and experience conferred by maturity, revives certain values of youth, first among these being freedom and a carefree attitude. After the difficulties of adult life, the inevitable sacrifices made for family and community, we are free at last and answerable to no one. There is a new world to conquer and explore. We can and must make up for lost time. Yes, life really does begin at 60.[5]

Let us take a look at the brochures targeting people in the third age, particularly those aimed at tourists. Everything about them radiates *joie de vivre* and the youth of mind and body. Some illustrations seem at first sight to have been designed for a quite different audience. Here is an idyllic scene on the deck of a yacht: he looks like a young executive on vacation; she, a blonde, could be his secretary. Yet, on closer inspection, we realize that this pair is actually a couple of 'old young people', no doubt husband and wife, on a voyage to some exotic island.

So the problem has been solved: there is no such thing as old age; it no longer exists. Its place has been taken by a specific form of youth. But there is no such thing as death either, and here we come to the final element in the strategy.

People in the third age seem too busy living really to die. Death comes afterwards. It happens in secret, beyond a certain limit that does not concern us.

In days gone by death was present all the time, both in reality and in people's minds. The moment of death was given great value. Everything took place in an edifying manner: people would die surrounded by their family. Death played a part in strengthening social ties, reinforcing solidarity between genera-tions and the link between earthly life and the hereafter.

In the contemporary model, by contrast, death is hidden. Philippe Ariès and Norbert Elias provide pertinent analyses of this phenomenon.[6] Once the 'exuberant' phase of the third age is over, old people are threatened with isolation. The healthy and forever young, created by the society of abundance, do not like to have the terminally ill or the dying near them. The third age, which begins as rediscovered youth, ends in the nursing home. After that the dying are whisked off to hospital, with the prospect of a discreet, sanitized, solitary end. Death is banished; it is confined to enclosed, strictly monitored spaces; it is invisible and so does not exist. It is always other people who die – it's their problem.

There is also a trend, particularly in the United States, to avoid prolonging life indefinitely, as can be done, even for the sick and old, thanks to our ever more effective medical technology. It is suggested, or indeed openly stated, that the infirm must make way for healthy individuals, for the truly alive.

This strategy, which can be summed up in the words 'We are young, death happens to other people, there's no such thing as death' has produced a new and comparatively effective reformulation of the myth of longevity. The illusion of perpetual youth goes hand in hand with a rejection of death, with a refusal to think about death, about one's own death.

Yet the purity of the model is tainted by darker realities. The spectre of AIDS, appearing at the very heart of the Western world in the 1980s, contributed to a new awareness of the real presence of suffering and death in a society ready to ignore them. Images of death come at us from all sides – scenes of famine and war, which, though generally occurring in faraway places, are projected right into our living-rooms. Their eradication seems to be no easy task. So while the myth continues to function, we cannot ask it for the impossible. It can give us no more than an imperfect illusion, which is already quite a lot.

LESS FOOD, MORE EXERCISE AND NO TOBACCO

Let us now move from the domain of appearances to that of effective strategies. We should start by looking close to home. There is a whole range of methods that everybody has always practised, whether consciously or not, in their everyday lives. Everyone eats and drinks in their own way, does more or less physical exercise and is more or less sexually active. Every day, without thinking about it, we help or hinder the process by which our own organism ages. These biological functions are at the same time highly socialized. Each cultural environment has its own habits in relation to food, sex and hygiene. It is not possible to make absolute judgements as to what is correct or incorrect. Neither the conclusions of science nor the prescriptions of medicine are immune from prejudice and fashion.

Today the watchword is 'less food' – fewer calories – if we want to live a little longer in good health. Having encouraged the consumption of excess food and calories, the consumer society is changing tack. Of course we must eat to live, but to live longer we must eat less.

Vegetarianism is on the increase in this context. In 1996, after seventeen years work, a group of British scientists confirmed the value of an essentially vegetarian diet. The hour of the Cretans has come. These island dwellers (and indeed Mediterranean peoples in general) eat fruit, vegetables and light meats (poultry and fish), avoiding animal fats. Cretan salad is particularly good; it seems to give the Cretans a solid life expectancy. They are, however, outdone by the inhabitants of the Japanese island of Okinawa, also fish-eating vegetarians, who hold the world record for life expectancy. So the case is proven.

According to certain (perhaps rather sadistic) scientists, the ideal diet is a little above the level of famine – a confirmation of Cornaro's views by today's science. This is not an easy path for today's Westerners to follow, given the temptations on offer where food is concerned.

An experiment is currently being carried out on monkeys that involves feeding various different groups differently, in order to observe the results (due in a decade or so). The underlying idea is, of course, that the monkeys that are fed the least will live the longest. As always, the sceptics take a dim view. They pity the poor animals condemned to suffer hunger and cold through lack of calories and wonder whether the means really justify the ends.

When mice were subjected to a similar regime they even lost the desire to mate. Here is something to look forward to! Already we can imagine human beings living a very long time in a state of total apathy. When they move from monkeys and rats to the human species, the number of calories really should be revised upwards. If we are to be condemned to live long, at least let our lives be bearable. The ideal would be somewhere between obesity (now sadly ever more common) and starvation. But the launch of an experiment using human volunteers has recently been announced, so we shall see.

The social standing of alcohol is also on the wane. From its origins in the United States the soft drinks offensive (whose supreme symbol is Coca-Cola) has advanced across the world. Wine is under direct threat. This has provoked a small 'war of the civilizations' between France and the United States. The French experts are seeking to rehabilitate wine, which they see as medicinal in the best sense, and are critical of sugary sodas. They take a similarly dim view of milk, beloved by the Nordic peoples: milk drinkers risk an early death. The paradoxical result is that, although the French are also fond of milk, their life expectancy is good because they reduce its negative effects by consuming quantities of wine (the fact is that, even in France, alcohol consumption has decreased in recent years, although the French remain champions in this respect). We should note that longevity sometimes wears national colours, at least where food and drink are concerned.[7]

Physical exercise is also strongly recommended, almost certainly because people are doing less and less. Our technological, information-based society, with its cars and computers, almost compels us to be sedentary. We need to do something to make up for this deficiency. Jogging has become a model practice in Western cultures, while people who walk a lot, take the stairs rather than the lift or practise a moderate amount of sport are credited with living longer.

One area that has seen radical change is that of attitudes towards smoking. Gently tolerated by earlier generations, tobacco is now condemned with no right of appeal. Of course you are still free to smoke, particularly if you want to die before time. Even Jeanne Calment gave up at the age of 117, a good example to the youth of today.

Smoking may be in decline, but sex is on the up. Today it is (almost) entirely guilt-free, the only fears to which it gives rise being strictly related to transmissible sexual diseases. Yet the fact that these – and particularly AIDS – are on the offensive is largely due to the liberation of sexual behaviour from Victorian taboos. Sex in itself is regarded as good for our health and mental equilibrium at any age. It is no longer cited as one of the presumed causes of premature ageing and death. If you are in your seventies and want to indulge in a 'vice', go for sex, not smoking.

We should also note – another feature of civilization – that the vogue for 'youth-giving diets' is generally linked to the fashion for diets to preserve the figure. These used to be mainly the preserve of women, but things are changing. Today growing numbers of men are also going on diets, particularly executives, worried about their real or apparent youth. They drink less wine and spirits and eat dietary products designed to help them lose weight. According to a recent study,

> restaurants must work with this new cult of the body. Gargantuan meals are a thing of the past. Almost all establishments with two or three Michelin stars offer 'low-calorie' menus or dishes [. . .] These clients, who tend to be business executives and industrialists, drink only water, even during business lunches. Such an attitude would have been unthinkable only ten years ago.[8]

Food is not the only aspect of life where things are changing. Men follow women in the gym; they are starting to follow them down the route of plastic surgery and are increasingly turning to beauty products. The 'forever young' phenomenon is on the move.

This new type of behaviour is highly instructive for anyone seeking to understand the amalgam of ideas surrounding longevity at the level of the imagination. Here we find a synthesis of three main elements: first, archetypal relationships of the kind that have long linked food and longevity; second, the latest scientific theories, including new research in the field of cellular biology, which I shall describe below; third, trends in the world of fashion, where the human type currently in favour is young, supple, relaxed and dynamic.

CELLULAR BIOLOGY AND GENETICS

The scientists have been at work, and this time it's for real. We are witnessing an all-out assault on death, led by cellular biology and genetics. By comparison the longevity strategies of 1900 look very primitive. Science has at last taken over, with corresponding results expected. The *New Scientist* sums up the new research with the title 'Death of Old Age'. 'Forever Young' says the cover of *Time*, where your eye meets that of an attractive young woman (perhaps one of tomorrow's young centenarians?)[9]

Scientists have identified cellular mechanisms that can explain the ageing process and suggest ways to fight it. These include the theory of oxidation, which sees ageing as a process of 'rusting', involving the same chemical reaction as that which alters iron or makes fire burn. The hunt is on for 'free radicals', elements produced when the cells are unable to break down part of the oxygen they have absorbed. The result is 'oxydizing stress', a series of reactions that can damage DNA and cellular structures as a whole.

'Forever Young',
the cover to
Time magazine
for 9 December
1996.

One highly recommended solution is a drastic reduction in calorie intake, in order to force the organism to 'burn' less food and go into a kind of slow motion. Here we have a scientific justification, derived from the study of cellular metabolism, for the need to combine a moderate intake of food with physical exercise. An even more direct solution is to take medication containing anti-oxidants (such as beta-carotene).

Also remarkable is the powerful comeback made by hormones, but in an incomparably more sophisticated context than that of Brown-Séquard's ram or Voronoff's monkeys. Hormone therapy

187

now has a wide-ranging arsenal at its disposal, including human growth hormone (HGH), which can be used to reinvigorate muscle tissue, and oestrogen, a hormone secreted by the ovaries, the level of which drops at menopause. A woman treated with oestrogen might gain an extra period of youth (resistance to some diseases, improved memory, more supple skin). Equivalent hormone therapy for men involves testosterone, the male sexual hormone, resulting in increased muscle and sexual appetite.

None, however, is so popular as DHEA, a steroid secreted by the suprarenal gland. The concentration of DHEA in the body reaches its peak when a person is about 25, after which it gradually declines until, around the age of 70, the body retains only 10 per cent of the amount it had in youth. The afflictions of old age are thought to result from this deficit. If the hypothesis turns out to be correct, treatment with DHEA might result in the reduction, and indeed eradication, of the problems of old age, including illnesses of all kinds, rheumatism, brittle bones and memory loss. The steroid DHEA has been freely sold (in pill form) in the USA since 1994, not as a medicine it is true, but with the less restrictive label of 'food supplement'. The Europeans are more reticent and doctors are divided between those 'for' and 'against'.

Last comes melatonin, a hormone secreted by the pineal gland and sometimes recommended in the treatment of stress and insomnia. Its anti-ageing effects (presumably due to the fact that its level drops at the age of around 50) are far from proven; however this has not prevented its remarkable success, explicable primarily by its low price. It flooded the American market in 1995 and can be bought in drugstores everywhere. The labels promise youth, health, sexuality, well-being and happiness, and all for $11. In a sign of the times, access to longevity has been democratized: with this new 'powdered youth', even the poor have a chance to stay young and become happy.

But there are two sides to every coin. Interventions designed to stimulate the organism can also (and perhaps more successfully) unbalance it. Growth hormone can foster diabetes and heart disease; oestrogen and testosterone increase the risk of cancer; the same goes for DHEA. The risks are often very real, while hopes remain problematic.

Those who are not in too much of a hurry might do better to wait for advances in genetics. This science has allowed us to explore the cogs of the 'clock of life', whose hands we may eventually be able to turn back. Particular attention is currently being paid to the ends of our chromosomes, known as the 'telomeres'. Whenever a cell divides, the telomeres get shorter; after 100 divisions there is almost nothing left of them and the cell can no longer reproduce. The best way to rejuvenate the cells might then be to give them a supplement of telomeres, which can be manipulated by means of an enzyme called 'telomerase', found in large doses in sperm and in cancer cells. The gene that gives rise to telomerase grants these cells a far greater capacity to divide, and thus to renew themselves, than that of ordinary cells, which explains, for example, the extraordinary growth of cancerous tissue. Here is an agent that, when properly controlled, might prolong the life of the organism by giving healthy cells the reproductive power of malignant tumours.

This argument is advanced in a book called *Reversing Human Ageing*, which caused a great stir on its publication early in 1996. Its author, an American doctor called Michael Fossel, is not one for circumspection. He states that very soon (and certainly before 2015) a therapy using telomerase will have been perfected, opening the door to a world in which people will live for hundreds of years. We are not quite there yet; putting the theory into practice will pose a few problems, such as whether each cell in the body should be injected, and if so, how? How will it be possible to avoid causing malfunctions and encouraging cancerous growth instead of providing the longed-for life expectancy?

Although its value for human beings remains as yet unproven, genetic manipulation seems to be providing real results in our more distant relatives. One of these is a minuscule species of worm, which has been treated in a Montreal laboratory. Known as the nematode worm, this creature has a natural life expectancy of no more than nine days; yet individuals used in the experiment have lived as long as 50 days. In human terms such an increase would give us 420 years instead of 80.

A series of experiments on fruit flies conducted by Michael Rose at the University of California, Los Angeles has given similar, if slightly more modest results. The insect subjects have lived as long as 130 days instead of 40. Turn these days into years and you have a human life expectancy extended across two centuries.

Of course the greatest hopes are linked to the human genome project. Exploration of our complete genetic system will make it possible to identify and control the mechanisms of disease and so, through gene therapy, to eradicate them. A life without illness would clearly be longer and, of course, infinitely better. Some experts believe this will soon be possible. Since genes seem to be specialized, possibly to a very high degree, some are even talking about genes responsible for the length of life. Effective action in this area would have almost unimaginable consequences; everything would become possible, including access to immortality.

Indeed the great news has come. In August 2001 American laboratories announced the identification of a chromosome ('chromosome 4') with the genetic characteristics of people who reach extreme old age. Might this be the discovery we've been waiting for?

At the moment, we must confess, the real problem is that there is too much to choose from in the way of recipes for longevity. More and more appear every day, and the prescriptions are almost never the same. The suppliers of long life all strongly recommend their own remedies and warn their customers against those of others. Here are some of the solutions on offer, taken from an extremely wide range. The choice is yours.

Roy Walford regards gerovital as useless; he gives no greater credence to the claims for the 'cellular therapy' practised by the Swiss doctor Paul Niehans, who injected fresh lamb's cells into several famous people, including Konrad Adenauer, Pope Pius XII and Winston Churchill (all of whom died prematurely in comparison to true centenarians). Instead Walford provides a long list of chemical and hormonal substances whose injection can be beneficial, while also recommending a diet based on the principle 'undernutrition without malnutrition', involving plenty of vegetables and very little salt. He could himself live 140 years, he says, were he to follow a diet close to the level of famine.

Gabriel Simonoff focuses on the highly remarkable properties of selenium, a chemical element present primarily in fish (which explains why the Japanese live so long), eggs and oils; it is also found in meat and bread, although in lesser proportions. So here we have our centenarians' menu. Sadly wine has not a trace of selenium: nor, to be fair, however, do water or milk. Pills are also available for the less greedy. 'For a long time', Simonoff confesses, 'I have swallowed a little selenium pill every day'. It would be worthwhile to keep an eye on the professor's career.[10]

On the sceptics' side, here are two passages from an interview given by Professor Karl-Heinz Krause, doctor-in-chief at the Hospital of Geriatrics in Geneva:

Do you prescribe DHEA to your patients? – No. I do not think it has any influence in preventing old age. It is no more than a false hope of eternal youth.

So what is the real secret of eternal youth? – The real miracle cure is (1) exercise, (2) not smoking, and (3) retaining (not losing) weight. These things are a hundred times more effective than DHEA and all the miracle cells![11]

However, the spiritual path is not entirely absent either. Despite growing secularization, religious piety and moral regeneration continue to supply the fountain of youth for some. The following extract illustrates such an attitude:

When man grows old [. . .] equilibrium breaks down and decrepitude comes. But all this is not the natural process of human life. It is because of his mentality and conduct that man grows old. He is not made for this. He is made to live on earth, in all the strength and power of eternal youth, which he can draw from the fount of life, the Most High.[12]

The divergent paths to immortality simply reflect the diverse beliefs and projects to be found among human beings today.

FREEZING, CLONES AND ROBOTS

Now let us raise the stakes and ask science to achieve even greater things – science or science fiction that is, assuming anyone can definitively distinguish between the two. For, as science advances, the ambitions and hopes it raises advance at the same rate; it would be naive to assume that current intellectual developments would lead to the depletion of our mythological store. On the contrary, today's science-based mythology is even richer and

'Cold Storage': freezing a client's body in a vat of liquid nitrogen at minus 370° Fahrenheit.

more varied than the religion-based mythology of our ancestors. This is because science is inexhaustible and our future plans have proliferated.

On the subject of achieving longevity we are currently witnessing an unprecedented boom in myth-creation. The more extreme methods, it is true, are reserved for a limited and preferably rich audience; for everything is becoming expensive in our world, including immortality.

Cold preserves things, this we know. Why should it not also preserve life? Apparently, according to some American scientists, a lower body temperature would help us to live longer. If, instead of 37°c, our bodies remained at only 35°c our life expectancy would increase to 140 years. A drop of seven degrees would enable us to reach the age of 200. In order to apply this attractive principle, one scientist had the idea of designing bedrooms as chill cabinets, able to reduce body temperature to 31 or 32°C.

Today's greatest hopes, however, are pinned on absolute cold. This method, known as cryogenics, was invented in the 1960s by the American physician Robert Ettinger (his first work on the subject, written in 1962, is explicitly entitled *The Prospect of Immortality*). The inventor's adolescence was strongly influenced by the adventures of a character we have already met: Professor Jameson. In this way *The Jameson Satellite* has provided the source for one of the most spectacular projects to achieve immortality ever put into practice: the suspension of the vital functions in the expectation that the patient will be revived in a more or less distant future (this is not the first time in our technological society that the path of science has passed through science fiction).

The principle is simple: when frozen at a very low temperature, the body remains unaltered for centuries, or even for eternity. People dying of incurable diseases – the most serious being death itself – can thus wait, in a stable state, for the day when medicine will have solved all their problems. That day may be near or far; time no longer matters to these time-travellers. The ethical and methodological problem then becomes one of deciding the right time to start the operation: it would not be appropriate to freeze someone who is still alive, or a corpse with no possibility of revival; action must be taken in the moments immediately following clinical death. That is the main concern for now; the rest is for the doctors of the future.

The candidates for immortality peacefully pass their time lying each in an individual cylinder at a constant temperature of −160°C. The world of tomorrow will benefit from a great infusion of millionaires, since the journey is far from free. The less wealthy rich are offered the possibility of preserving only their heads, in less voluminous capsules. What does the trunk matter, as long as you still have your head? (We should moreover remember that the Zoromes kept only the head of Professor Jameson.) This branch of the refrigeration industry is doing good business in the United States, particularly in California, to the benefit of its patients and entrepreneurs alike.

However, such procedures may ultimately prove rather crude. In reality a single cell contains all the biological information necessary to crack the genetic code, enabling the entire organism to be faithfully reconstructed. This was the technique used by Michael Crichton and Steven Spielberg to make the dinosaurs walk again. When will we see it applied to human beings, so that we can each use our own cells to perpetuate ourselves into infinity?

Another revolutionary project now taking shape involves growing new organs to replace worn-out parts of the human body. The simplest are already in use, for example in grafts of skin cells grown on polymer substrata. It has even been possible to 'manufacture' a human ear (on a mouse). In a few decades it will be possible to make more complex organs such as hands, kidneys and hearts. The more optimistic scientists believe that after 2050 every organ in the human body will be replaceable, apart from the brain.[13]

This leads us directly to human cloning. As the technique of cloning has already been mastered, the only remaining obstacles are of an ethical nature. It is in your interests to have your own clone (or possibly several). For what purpose? Why, as an organ bank of course. Your alter ego would provide you with a complete set of organs absolutely identical to your own. Any part of your body that became subject to disease could be replaced immediately by a healthy part, enabling you to upgrade your body in perpetuity. We should clarify, to settle your scruples, that your clone would be programmed to have no consciousness of any kind; it would be a purely vegetative creature, a 'human cabbage' designed exclusively to keep its original supplied with fresh organs and tissue.

If you care more about your mind than your body, you can have yourself transferred to a computer. Artificial intelligence is advancing at such a pace that we can already imagine a time when its networks will be at least as complex as those of the human brain. Everything contained in your brain cells – memory, intelligence, emotions – could be absorbed by the electronic brain of a robot that would, of course, retain your personality. True, this solution is more akin to a technological version of the spiritual immortality of religion than to bodily immortality. We can think of it as a new kind of metempsychosis: when you die you will come back as a robot.

THE LATEST NEWS FROM CHINA

Interesting news has recently come in from China.[14] The Chinese have a tradition of longevity, so it is only natural that it should continue to flourish. It is moreover hard to judge how much of the following information is authentically Chinese and how much reflects the process of selection and orientation to which it has been subjected on arrival here. Saturated with technology, the West sometimes likes to escape into exotic spaces where nature still rules and miracles occur quite naturally, as they did in the good old days.

The recent Chinese news chiefly concerns the curious phenomenon of 'third teeth'. In 1982 a Shanghai daily newspaper described the case of a centenarian peasant from the south of the country, who 'was astounded one fine morning to see twenty new teeth growing in his jaws'. The story was repeated in 1988 with an old man from north-western China, whose teeth re-grew dramatically in one night. Lastly, in 1994, a slightly younger Chinese woman got her teeth back at the age of 92.

It is the speed that is impressive: in China teeth grow in the space of a night. Otherwise this sign of rejuvenation has been well known for a long time. At the moment it seems there is no threat to the absolute record, recorded by Hufeland and held by a German who died in 1791 at the age of 120. In his last four years, this man had the good fortune to grow no fewer than 50 new teeth.

Such 'third teeth' usually appear in tandem with other signs of youth, and sometimes with almost total rejuvenation. The most remarkable case was recorded in 1983. A Chinese woman of 110 suddenly began to grow younger. Eight new teeth appeared in her jaws and 'part of her white hair became black again, while her wrinkled skin became supple and glowing once more'; even more remarkably, 'her menstrual cycle returned and her face became covered in juvenile acne'.

Lastly, a piece of news put out in 1994 returns to the old theme of the fountain of youth. A recently discovered well was said to have enabled an octogenarian couple from north-eastern China to enjoy a second youth. Their wrinkles disappeared and the man, who had been bald, regained a fine head of brown hair.

EXTRATERRESTRIALS

From China to the world of the extraterrestrials is but a short step. Extraterrestrial life has the function of providing us with answers to every imaginable question, including, of course, those relating to the length of life. While extreme longevity poses a few difficulties for human beings on Earth, there is nothing to stop extraterrestrials from living thousands of years and even, in extreme cases, enjoying immortality. In his *Histoire comique des Etats et Empires de la Lune* ('Comic History of the States and Empires of the Moon', published posthumously in

1657), Cyrano de Bergerac describes the Solarians, who live for 3,000 or 4,000 years, reincarnating themselves by turns on Earth or the moon. Here is the seed of the combined theme of longevity and cosmic travel that Professor Jameson's Zoromes merely refined.

An important threshold was crossed in 1947 with the observation of the first flying saucers. Hitherto extraterrestrials had been present only in the imaginations of philosophers and writers; now they had appeared among us. They became a presence. There was a proliferation of encounters of the 'third kind'. Men and women were 'contacted'; some found themselves, willingly or otherwise, taken into the space ships of these creatures from elsewhere. Extraterrestrials also provided food for beliefs of a religious provenance, beginning to compete with God up in Heaven. To those who believe in them they offer the way to salvation; at least so say the 'flying saucerist' sects that have proliferated in recent decades.

The subject of extraterrestrials is vast. I offer a single example, chosen for its close links to the theme of longevity. A Frenchman named Claude Vorilhon was contacted by a species of extraterrestrials of human appearance, but far more developed than humanity on Earth. Following this revelation he founded the 'Raëlian' movement and began to preach the good news, passing on messages he had received from the other world. This is what 'they' have to say about our theme:

Our body lives on average ten times as long as yours, like the first men of the Bible. Between 750 and 1,200 years. But our spirit, thus our true character, can be truly immortal. I have explained to you that using any cell of the body we can recreate the entire being with new living matter: when we have all our faculties and our brain is at the height of its powers and knowledge, we have a tiny part of our bodies surgically removed and preserved. When we actually die, we use a cell, taken from the small part of our body that was removed, to completely re-create our body as it was at that time. I say as it was at that time, in other words with the same personality and scientific knowledge it had then. However the body is made from new elements that have 1,000 of your years before them to live. And so on for eternity. Except that, in order to keep the population down, only geniuses have a right to eternity.

There follows some interesting information about the daily lives of these 'immortals':

'How do you live and work?'
'In practice we work only intellectually, since our scientific level allows us to use robots for everything. We work only when we feel like it and only with our brains.'
'But if you live such a long time and don't work, don't you get bored?'
'No, never, Since we all do the things we like, and in particular we make love. We find our women very beautiful and enjoy them.'[15]

So there it is, not a bad lifestyle. Most importantly, these distant cousins of ours have plans for us. They want the Earth to take up the torch of their civilization one day. When they come to die, their science will automatically be transmitted to us. Unfortunately that will not be for some time.

It may be that things will move fast, however. In December 2002 the Raëlians announced the birth of the first human clone. They seem determined to establish on earth the model they have taken from extraterrestrials.

The quest for longevity does not focus exclusively on biology. It also opens the door to a new utopia. We were much in need of one. The social myths forged in modern times are coming to the end of their useful lives. The communist dream has faded and capitalism goes on functioning without generating much enthusiasm, for lack of a better alternative. The twenty-first century needs to reinvent civilization, perhaps by means of longevity.

The fact is that lives are lengthening while the birth-rate is going down. In the West the number of deaths is about to equal, if not surpass, that of births. The other regions of the world will probably follow the Western trend. So we are evolving towards societies where the elderly will represent an ever-growing percentage of the population. Eventually the active population may become smaller than the category of retired people it is required to support. If everyone lives to be around 120, and assuming today's arrangements remain the norm, we will spend 60 years in retirement, compared to 40 years of working life.

If we are to make a success out of living longer, 'old people' will have to change. All we can say is that, at present, older people are getting younger only up to a point; beyond that any extension of life goes hand in hand with infirmity and illness (such as the sadly familiar Alzheimer's disease). The goal of the longevity quest, however, assumes a vigorous old age, or rather an extension of life without old age or disease. Ideally the man of 120 or 150 will be almost as young as his grandsons. This is the great challenge, for both biology and society. If it is successfully met, the result will be the total transformation of human life.

No one's career will come to an end at 60; instead the retirement age will be set according to life expectancy; with an active life of 100 years or so it may even be possible to have two or three successive careers. People's personal lives will no doubt also be restructured, making way for intergenerational marriages and 'polygenerational' families. This will surely be a more varied and interesting world than our own, allowing all individuals to fulfil their own potential and turn their dreams into reality.

A new social system and new social relations will emerge. The journalist Louis Bériot undertook a huge international study to identify the outlines of this new world in gestation, publishing the results as *Le Grand Défi: Tous centenaires et en bonne santé* ('The Great Challenge: All Centenarians and in Good Health', 1991). The revelations offered in this work are fascinating: both humanity and civilization are in the process of radical change.

Right at the start the author states that 'longevity and reduced fertility represent a new opportunity for the world and the Earth'. There will be more older people, but they will be healthy and active (including sexually), while numbers of young people will fall. Human relations and human life in general will be reinvented as a result. Men will be less aggressive and less hasty. Women, freed of the tasks demanded by large traditional families, will occupy an important place in society. Life will be richer and more enjoyable: thinking, inventing and making love will be the main occupations. Whatever else, the problems posed by global overpopulation will certainly be a thing of the past, and there will at least be fewer candidates for unemployment.

We are undoubtedly right to be worried by the prospect of a society in which there are more centenarians than children and young people, despite the promised advantages. Yet the fact remains that such a society would seem the logical outcome of today's global trends, in which myth and reality meet.

In 2001 Michael Rose, the fruit fly specialist, made a resounding declaration: 'I believe there are already immortal people.' You would think it was Shaw speaking: so some of our contemporaries are already 'immortal', without appearing different in any way and without being aware of it themselves. In more moderate vein another longevity expert, Steve Austad of the University of Idaho, proposed a bet that some people alive today would still be alive and active in 2150. If he is one of the chosen few, not only will he have the satisfaction of being right, he will also pocket all the money.

However, while enthusiasm may be soaring on one side, scepticism is stating its case no less clearly on the other. What do the sceptics have to say?[16]

In the first place they observe that we risk falling victim to an illusion concerning increases in life expectancy over the last century. From 45 to almost 80 years is truly spectacular. The statistics for 1900, however, were affected by a particularly high rate of infant mortality. Since then the averages have risen because children and young people are much less likely to die, so any actual lengthening of life has a relatively minor role in the calculation. Life expectancy is already rising more slowly, now that the rates of infant mortality and adult deaths 'before time' have dropped to such a low level that we can expect little more in that direction. From now on any observable gains will have to be made by the old, and every extra year will be a real struggle. There is no question of living 120 years in the near future; even to reach the more modest figure of 100 years, medicine would have to eliminate today's common causes of death, which it is not about to do.

Secondly, the sceptics do not accept the rather weak analogies between the human organism and those of the worms and insects that have responded so promptly to longevity treatments; already experiments on mice have proved less conclusive. The complexity of human biology makes things complicated. Nematode worms and fruit flies have the good fortune not to develop cancer or Alzheimer's disease.

The widely recommended method of eating frugally in order to accumulate fewer calories and reduce numbers of 'free radicals' does not seem to have been scientifically proven either. We still have to wait some years for the definitive results of experiments carried out on monkeys (and recently repeated on human volunteers). However, intermediate tests indicate that the current monkey subjects are ageing at the usual pace. That would really put the icing on the cake: never eating your fill, suffering from the cold and spending all your time vegetating in a state of apathy just to gain a few extra years, and then ultimately gaining none.

The effects of hormones are equally uncertain. While tens of thousands of Americans are treating themselves with growth hormone, scientists confess that they have no definite knowledge about its rejuvenating effects (they know perhaps a little more about the cancer risks involved in such treatment). Some voices have been heard to suggest that this hormone may in fact shorten rather than lengthen life. At the same time experiments have shown that people with a hormone deficit do not necessarily die any younger than the rest. The prestige of hormones as 'elixirs of life' or 'fountains of youth' seems somewhat inappropriate.

The baby of the 'anti-ageing' campaign, 'chromosome 4', is not immune from criticism either. For while this chromosome has undeniably been found in half the centenarians tested, the fact remains that it is not present in the other half.

Life is a very complicated thing, and prolonging it even more so. We are left with one piece of good news, however: the struggle for longevity goes on.

Conclusions

This book is not about longevity itself, but about longevity in the world of the imagination, which is not quite the same thing. I have not sought to separate what is true from what is not – still less to predict the future of the human race; I have simply traced the path of an idea down the centuries. While the real questions in the longevity debate remain open, the subject has the merit of revealing how an archetype functions. What could be more elementary, more inherent in human nature, than the desire to avoid death, to cheat it, or delay it as long as possible?

The range of methods for prolonging life is very wide, as is the range of ways to live longer. However, such diversity is based on simple, durable structures. The more modest proposals focus strictly on managing the span of our lives as well as possible by eliminating disease, maintaining our physical and intellectual faculties and enjoying a vigorous old age, without these improvements leading necessarily to an 'extension'. The idea of the natural limit is also challenged, but should it be 70 or 80 years, 100 or even 120? The door remains open to a gradual increase in life expectancy. As for the more audacious plans, all are versions of three or four scenarios involving either true longevity (with ever higher ceilings: 120 years, 150, 200, several hundred and indeed several thousand years), immortality, or, in two distinct variants, perpetual youth and rejuvenation. Of course these scenarios may be

combined: longevity stretches towards immortality and sometimes even gets there; it also assumes perpetual youth or constant
rejuvenation, at least for some attributes. The balance differs from
one case to the next: some may live for a century, others for eternity, some remain perfectly youthful while others have their youth
restored; some preserve or regain only one important element of
youthful energy (sexual potency, new teeth). A distinction should
also be made between pure mythology and real strategies. Some
simply dream of inaccessible longevity (golden age, distant lands,
extraterrestrials), while others seek to act on their dreams (though
in practice the division between the two registers remains fluid:
all fiction also assumes an intention and any practical action has
its source in a projected ideal).

The means employed (in both imagination and reality) seem
inexhaustible. Ultimately anything can be used to prolong and
improve life. Water, blood, cinnabar, the elixir of life, eating plants,
purgations, oil, electricity, glands and hormones, the soul, reason,
monkeys' testicles, the Bogomoletz serum, gerovital, heat and
cold, DHEA and telomerase, Bulgarian yoghurt and young girls all
figure on an endless and apparently incoherent list. Yet this list is
in fact entirely coherent since, let us repeat, anything can be used
to prolong life. The means mentioned here and a considerable
number of others are interchangeable or complementary.

Modern science has brought substantial changes in method, but
it has kept in place a series of traditional symbols. One example
is blood, the principle of life. The regenerative powers of blood
manifest themselves in countless hypostases – the blood of Christ
caught in the Holy Grail, blood-red cinnabar, or vampires feeding
on the blood of the living – and it continues to play a similar role
today in the context of a more technological process, in so far as
transfusions of young blood seem able to rejuvenate the organism.
Vegetarianism was originally inspired by religious and ethical

values; more recent arguments of a medical nature confirm its regenerative powers, which have been symbolized since time immemorial by the vital force of plants.

Sometimes the new methods seem very remote from the ancient legends, but in fact they are suprisingly close. Obviously the endocrine glands do not figure in the traditional arsenal of longevity. Their function is nevertheless exactly the same as that fulfilled in bygone days by means today regarded as fictitious or untrustworthy. In the contemporary imagination transplants represent the fountain of youth or elixir of life. The techniques are very different; yet these remain of secondary importance in relation to their supposed results, which always remain the same.

The following example seems minor, but is not without significance. A cartoon strip from 1950 (called *Death Must Come!*, by Al Feldstein) drew on the possibilities offered by transplants, whose career in the scientific imagination was just beginning. Frederick and Henry, two newly qualified doctors, discover that youth can be prolonged by replacing a gland in the spleen with a younger one. Henry operates on Frederick four times at intervals of several years; the bodies necessary are dug up from the cemetery. At the age of 75 Frederick still looks like a young man of 25. But his friend refuses to repeat the operation. There is a fight and Henry dies from a heart attack. Frederick decides to carry out the operation himself. He kills a boy, but realizes to his horror that his victim has had the part of his spleen that contains the necessary gland removed. It is too late to find another solution. In a few minutes Frederick rapidly ages and dies.

This is an undoubtedly modern tale: it is told in cartoon form, involves the regenerative function of the endocrine glands and transplants, and its atmosphere of violence and horror are very much of its century. All the details are modern, yet this cannot prevent a feeling of *déjà vu*. We recall the old story of the traveller who discovers perpetual youth, then returns to his own country, where time speeds up, so that he suffers ageing and inevitable death in a few moments. Such stories remind us that we are implacably fated to die. Eternal youth cannot protect us. We may cheat old age, we may temporarily cheat time, but we can never cheat death.

We can only conclude that man continually reinvents the same stories, changing nothing but the setting. The sombre, or at least sceptical, moral of the above example raises another question, that of the myth's ambiguity. It has an optimistic message to the extent that longevity signifies a victory – however temporary – over time, decrepitude and death. Yet we must also look at the other side of the coin. Every plan for attaining longevity bears the image of death like a watermark. Usually any overt optimism is no more than the sometimes uneasy counterpart of an existential despair that remains with man throughout his existence. We invent ways of achieving longevity in order to forget, for a second, the void that surrounds us. The human inability to accept our limited condition and, ultimately, our own death defines the tragic nature of our existence. The quest for longevity speaks of both man's Promethean ambitions and his fundamental impotence.

Ironically and, at the same time, tragically, it seems human beings are destined to fear both death and eternity in equal measures. Life without end would be a crushing burden. Immortals would come to dream of death just as mortals dream of immortality.

In a sign of the times, some recent trends have been, to varying extents, more favourable to the indefinite prolongation of life. The conquest of time can also be combined with that of space. In an infinite universe of inexhaustible variety, immortals would no longer have time to become bored, as they once did, when they were confined to a few acres of Earth. The last word has yet to be spoken, but the problem remains: delaying death will not be enough; people will also have to show themselves capable of 'managing' their near-eternity.

In this context we should note the highly elitist version of immortality, in which the privilege is reserved for a 'cast' invested with wisdom and power. Such a solution was suggested by Čapek and put into practice by the extraterrestrials close to the Raëlian movement.

It is also interesting to observe how the models have migrated. Originally located at the dawn of time, in the modern period longevity has become a thing of the future. In traditional societies it illustrates the gradual fall of man; today, conversely, it is proof of the progress made by the species. Long life was once received as a gift from the gods or from nature, although some may have tried to obtain it through their own science; today it is becoming an exclusively human conquest, demonstrating man's capacity to act on himself and to modify his own substance. All the signposts have been reversed. Everything is different and yet everything is the same. The golden age has simply been projected into the future and man has taken the place of the Creator, while longevity, immortality and youth remain at the myth's unchanging core.

Grand centenarians like to keep their distance. They gather at the two ends of history, the distant past and future, and at the ends of the world, or at least in countries with a certain exotic stamp. The Greeks favoured India, the far North and Ethiopia. In medieval Europe the British Isles enjoyed a fine reputation as a home to centenarians, explicable by both their indigenous folklore and their island state and geographical eccentricity. This tradition lasted right into the modern period, at which point the fabulously old were hounded out of Western Europe by the registrars, regrouping under the more clement skies of the East. Bulgaria and Russia took full advantage of their presence, sharing the glory with other countries located primarily in Asia and Latin America. In the twentieth century the Caucasus, Pakistan and Ecuador have shared the absolute records – unless we count the visitors from other galaxies.

A strong tradition always has a purpose. How can we explain the multitude of Russian contributions, from the likes of Metchnikoff, Voronoff, Bogomoletz and a whole host of Soviet scientists, other than by the indestructibility of the myth's roots? Their 'scientific' arguments no doubt owe a great deal to the massive presence of centenarians in the collective imagination, if not in the demographic reality of the country. The British Isles enjoy a no less exceptional tradition; for centuries they provided the most successful examples of centenarians in the Western world, as well as the first systematic research into prolonging life. It is quite natural then that the debate on longevity should have continued into the modern period, with particularly strong opinions being expressed on either side. More exemplary still is the case of China, where recent manifestations of mythical longevity are part of a tradition several thousand years old.

While respectful of tradition, the 'science' of longevity also likes to keep up with the latest fashions. It teaches people how to live long lives, which in practice means 'how life should be lived'. However the prescription for how life should be lived differs greatly from one period and one culture to the next.

Nothing could be more instructive in this respect than the dietary approach to longevity, which is worthy of detailed study. There are almost no foodstuffs of any importance that have not been judged, either successively or simultaneously, to be good or bad for health, capable of prolonging or, conversely, shortening life. Entirely contradictory medical arguments have been advanced on this subject; we have learned that it is both good and bad to consume meat, bread or wine. Fashions change, pass and return. The principle alone remains the same, in other words the idea – as deeply rooted now as it was in the days of Hippocrates – that our health ultimately depends on what we eat. Fortunately, we can always swap one dish for another, with scientific arguments to back up our choice. Science and fashion are old friends.

Fashion leads us directly to cultural synthesis and ideology. The subject of longevity is highly revealing, inviting us to embark on a process of cultural and ideological decoding. In the course of this discussion it has enabled us to identify certain particular traits in four types of civilization: Greco-Roman antiquity is both pragmatic and resigned to fate; China seeks wisdom and presents a particularly 'internalized' model of life; the medieval West invents a transcendent version of progress; the modern West translates progress into effective, material terms.

In the social and political game longevity appears as a mark of superiority, of biological and social prestige. It has long been used as an argument to support royal and religious authorities and was called for by the Renaissance and the Enlightenment as a means to emancipate the mind and body. Men long saw it as an additional indicator of their superiority over women. The opposing elitist and democratic values of recent centuries have in their turn made periodic appeal to the same argument. The life of savages and civilization, pure country air and urban facilities have been valued and devalued according to ideological criteria. The rich and poor both receive their just deserts, in contradictory mythological versions. The oft-recommended frugal life is perfectly suited to the poor, while a more succulent diet is proposed for the rich, who also have other advantages including, most recently, travel into the future in refrigerated capsules.

An increasing density of contradictory solutions reflects increasing tension in the social organism. A striking example of this is provided by the inter-war period, where the search for longevity grew more complex because history itself was becoming more complex; the ideologues were in charge, each with their own approach to biological perfection.

In the contemporary West on the other hand, where ideologies are fading, it is individualism that is most frequently expressed through the quest for longevity. At the same time an extremely wide range of individual solutions is increasingly interfering with an emergent utopia involving the reshaping of the human condition. The quest for longevity seems destined to thrust twenty-first-century humanity into a very different world from that we know now. It is taking the place of the transformist ideologies, which did not keep their promises. This time we'll get there, thanks to genetics.

All approaches are of equal worth: the myth's continuity is impressive. From antiquity to the present day longevity has taken countless shapes, yet in its essence it has proved fairly stable. Even the numbers remain the same: 100 years, 120 (Moses's age), 150, 200. On the other hand what has changed radically is the practice of increasing longevity. From the end of the Middle Ages to the present day, 'Western man' has never been content with imagination alone. He has turned his dreams into action. The ways of achieving longevity are constantly proliferating, growing more ambitious at every stage; they shed light on the thirst for knowledge and conquest that characterizes modern Western civilization, its will to transform and its determination to conquer nature, including human nature.

One last, and particularly delicate, question remains: is 'extreme' longevity just a myth, no more than a chimera that man has been hunting pointlessly for thousands of years?

On this matter it is important to keep the levels separate. Mythology and the real world have independent, parallel existences. They are linked by continual and meaningful exchanges, but these relationships do not change their specific essences. Clearly myth influences human behaviour; the obsessive quest for longevity, and indeed immortality, has manifested itself in the search for effective solutions, and will endlessly continue to do so. These include methods for achieving what is regarded as 'natural' longevity (which quickly slips from 100 years to the next stage of 120) and those aiming at a far greater longevity, which necessitates the reconstruction of human biology. A constant increase in life expectancy may justify both these approaches at the same time. It can be interpreted as an unbroken march that no barrier can halt; it may also be interpreted as a kind of democratization, enabling a larger number of people to approach an uncrossable biological limit (similar to the phenomenon of increasing height; there are more and more tall people, but this evolution does not seem to presage a world in which people will be three or four metres tall).

One unavoidable element in the quest for longevity is the 'redistribution' of the ages of life. To extend our days essentially by prolonging old age (even in improved form) is not an attractive proposition. Might Swift be right? What is the point of living for eternity in an ever more advanced state of decrepitude? For the moment the results remain ambiguous. Despite an infusion of (real or apparent) youth, the specific ills of the third age are far from eliminated (indeed they are more present, given the increased number of people reaching an advanced age). It may be a little early to tell Swift that he was wrong.

In reality the chances of success have nothing in common with the myth. Whether real or illusory, they remain completely independent. Many of our contemporaries like to believe in extraterrestrials, yet this myth in no way affects the existence or non-existence of the inhabitants of the galaxies. The myth of longevity follows the same logic; it has nothing to tell us about the future development of our species. The imaginary exploration of the future is something quite different from the future itself, that unknown and as yet undiscovered territory. Everything remains possible, but the real future is unlikely to resemble that of our imagination. So will we become immortal or not? Our descendants will be the ones to know.

The fact is that people will never abandon the project to reinvent the human condition. Our desire to be different is deeply ingrained in our spiritual structure; it is an archetypal constant; we are 'programmed' that way. Although archetypes can change shape or slot into different strategies, in their essence they are always themselves. Whether divine creatures or creators of gods, human beings continue to search for transcendent solutions to enable them to reach a higher state. Longevity was and will always be a crucial element in the interminable confrontation between man and God, the human struggle to appropriate a piece of divinity, the ultimate goal of which is to transform human beings into human gods.

References

Because this book is an overview of the subject, rather than a specialist scholarly study, I have kept notes to the minimum necessary. In most cases works cited in the text have not been included in the notes. My sole aim is to provide the reader with the essential information succinctly and, where necessary, to give the sources of some quotations.

INTRODUCTION

1 For an overview of ideas on longevity (up to the end of the eighteenth century), see Gerald J. Gruman's highly documented study *A History of Ideas about the Prolongation of Life: The Evolution of Prolongevity Hypotheses to 1800*, published as a complete work in *Transactions of the American Philosophical Society*, new series, LVI/9 (1966). An abundantly illustrated synthesis was published with the title *Search for Immortality* (Alexandria, VA, 1992). I should also mention my own preliminary essay on the question: Lucian Boia, *Pour vivre deux cents ans: Essai sur le mythe de la longévité* (Paris, 1998).

1 ORIGINAL PERFECTION

1 The Methuselah file (with its related considerations of longevity) is the subject of J. P. Bois, 'Mathusalem, l'homme le plus vieux', *Bulletin de la Société archéologique de Nantes et de Loire-Atlantique* (1994–5), pp. 17–29
2 On the theory of progress in general and the inability of the

Ancients to accept it fully, see two classic texts: J. B. Bury, *The Idea of Progress* (London, 1920) and E. R. Dodds, *The Greeks and the Irrational* (Berkeley, 1951). I also return here to some of the arguments I advanced in Lucian Boia, *La Fin du monde: Une histoire sans fin* (Paris, 1989, repr. 1999).

3 In describing the edges of the world I have drawn on the description I gave in *Entre l'Ange et la Bête: Le Mythe de l'Homme différent de l'Antiquité à nos jours* (Paris, 1995), pp. 43–4. On the world system as imagined by the Greeks, see François Hartog's crucial work, *Le Miroir d'Hérodote: Essai sur la représentation de l'autre* (Paris, 1980).

4 Herodotus, *Histories* III.20–23.

5 *Ibid.* I.216.

6 The Greeks' knowledge of India owed a great deal to the stories of Ctesias (fifth century BC) and Megasthenes (early third century BC), of which only fragments remain. For an overview of the wonders of India, see Lucian Boia, *Entre l'Ange et la Bête*, pp. 49–52.

7 The longevity of the Hyperboreans is mentioned by Strabo (*Geography* xv.i.57), who criticizes the information on this people provided by Megasthenes.

8 The story of Iambulus is recounted by Diodorus Siculus, *Historical Library* II.55–60.

9 Monique Halm-Tisserant, *Cannibalisme et immortalité: L'Enfant dans le chaudron en Grèce ancienne* (Paris, 1993).

10 On Daoism and its techniques to achieve longevity, see Gerald J. Gruman's detailed presentation, *A History of Ideas about the Prolongation of Life*, pp. 28–49. I have also drawn on Max Kaltenmark, *Lao-tseu et le Taoisme* (Paris, 1965).

11 Herodotus, *Histories* III.23.

12 A very useful work in relation to the debate around longevity in Greco-Roman antiquity is the collective work on old age, *Senectus: La vecchiaia nel mondo classico*, ed. Umberto Mattioli (Bologna, 1995), I: *Grecia*, II: *Roma*

13 Umberto Mattioloi, 'Ambigua aetas', in *Senectus: La vecchiaia nel mondo classico*, I, pp. x–xiii.

14 'Introduction' to Roger Bacon, *De retardatione accidentium*

senectutis, ed. A. G. Little and E. Withington (Oxford, 1928), p. xxxvi.

15 Seneca, *Letters to Lucilius* I, letter xii, 6.

16 *Ibid.*, IX, letter 77, 19.

17 Lucretius, *De rerum natura*, end of Book III.

18 Pliny the Elder, *Natural History* VII.48–9.

19 B. Baldwin, *Studies in Lucian* (Toronto, 1973), p. 25.

20 St Augustine, *The City of God*, xv, 12.

21 *Ibid.*, xv, 14.

22 *Ibid.*, xv, 15.

23 *Ibid.*, xv, 9.

24 *Ibid.*, XIII, 23; XXII, 15.

25 Aristotle, *De generatione animalium*. On Aristotle's opinions, see also Giordana Pisi, 'La medicina greca antica' in *Senectus: La vecchiaia nel mondo classico*, I, pp. 469–77.

2   BY THE GRACE OF GOD

1 Jacques Le Goff, 'L'Occident médiéval et l'océan Indien: Un horizon onirique', in *Pour un autre Moyen Age* (Paris, 1977), pp. 280–98.

2 These records are listed in the article on 'Longévité', *Grand Dictionnaire universel du XIXe siècle*, ed. Pierre Larousse (Paris, 1866–76), x, p. 663. For a critical reconstruction of these biographies, see David Hugh Farmer, *Oxford Dictionary of Saints* (Oxford, 1992).

3 Georges Minois, *Histoire de la vieillesse en Occident: De l'Antiquité à la Renaissance* (Paris, 1987), p. 234.

4 I found this story in Amédée Thierry, *Histoire d'Attila et de ses successeurs* (Paris, 1856), which, despite its 'age', is still of interest for its collection of legends concerning Attila and the Huns.

5 My main reference was Pseudo-Callisthenes, *Le Roman d'Alexandre*, trans. and annotated Gilles Bounoure and Blandine Serret (Paris, 1992). Bounoure's introduction, pp. ix–xxxviii, reviews the research on the filiation of this group of texts.

6 For Mandeville I have drawn on the work of Christiane Deluz, *Le Livre de Jehan de Mandeville: Une géographie au XIVe siècle*

(Louvain-la-Neuve, 1988) and her editions of Mandeville's text: *Voyage autour de la terre* (Paris, 1993) and *Le Livre des merveilles du monde* (Paris, 2000).

7 An excellent introduction to Irish mythology can be found in Daragh Smyth, *A Guide to Irish Mythology* (Dublin, 1988).

8 *Ibid.*, p. 122.

9 This tale is analysed in Jacques Le Goff's article, 'Aspects savants et populaires des voyages dans l'au-delà au Moyen Age', in *L'Imaginaire médiéval* (Paris, 1985), pp. 112–14.

10 This Romanian tale, 'Tinereţe fără bătrîneţe şi viaţă fără de moarte', can be found in Petre Ispirescu's collection, *Legende sau basmele românilor* (Bucharest, 1872–6); an English translation, 'Youth Everlasting and Life without End', appears in *Tales and Stories* (London and Bucharest, 1975).

11 For alchemy and the relationship between alchemy and longevity, see Gerald J. Gruman, 'The Alchemists' in *A History of Ideas about the Prolongation of Life*, pp. 49–68, and Serge Hutin, *L'Immortalité alchimique* (Paris, 1991).

12 An excellent account of Bacon's system to achieve longevity can be found in the 'Introduction' to *De retardatione accidentium senec'tutis*, II ['Characteristics. Authorities. System. Occult Remedies. Estimate'], ed. A. G. Little and E. Withington (Oxford, 1928), pp. XXXI–XLIV.

3 THE BODY STRIKES BACK

1 This story is told by Christoph Wilhelm Hufeland in *Makrobiotik, oder die Kunst das menschliche Leben zu verlängern* (Jena, 1796).

2 An excellent presentation of the wonders of America can be found in Jorge Magasich-Airola and Jean-Marc de Beer, *America Magica: Quand l'Europe de la Renaissance croyait conquérir le Paradis* (Paris, 1994); on longevity, see pp. 64–73.

3 This poem appears in *Dichtungen von Hans Sachs*, I (Leipzig, 1870), pp. 268–70.

4 Note taken from Hufeland, *Makrobiotik*.

5 A complete discussion of Descartes and longevity can be found in Gruman, *A History of Ideas about the Prolongation of Life*,

pp. 77–80.

6   Victor Hugo includes this rumour in *Les Misérables*, III ('Marius'),
    Book 1, chapter VI.

7   Hufeland, *Makrobiotik*.

4   REASON WORKS MIRACLES

1   In this chapter I return to arguments I have developed in
    two earlier books: on the reconstruction of myth in the
    Enlightenment, see *Pour une histoire de l'imaginaire* (Paris, 1998),
    pp. 60–64; on biological imagery in the same period, see *Entre
    l'Ange et la Bête*, pp. 109–72.

2   Detailed biographical information on these three figures is
    provided in *Biographie universelle ancienne et moderne* [*Biographie
    Michaud*] (Paris, 1842–65): Cagliostro (VI), Mesmer (XXVIII), Saint-
    Germain (XXXVII).

3   Buffon's ideas on human biology, including longevity, are in the
    section 'De l'homme' of *Histoire naturelle*. For the history of life
    in general, see his work *Les Epoques de la nature* (Paris, 1778),
    particularly Jacques Roger's introduction to the critical edition
    of this work (Paris, 1962).

4   This fragment of Franklin's letter is taken from Gruman,
    A History of Ideas about the Prolongation of Life, p. 74.

5   THE AGE OF THE SCIENTIFIC UTOPIA

1   'Longévité', *Grand Dictionnaire*, X, p. 663.

2   *Ibid.*

3   Jean-François Braunstein, 'Auguste Comte, la Vierge Marie
    et les vaches folles: Les Utopies biomédicales du positivisme',
    in *L'Utopie de la santé parfaite: Colloque de Cérisy*, ed. Lucien Sfez
    (Paris, 2001), pp. 298–9.

4   The Faust dossier is presented in detail by André Dabezies in
    Le Mythe de Faust (Paris, 1972, repr. 1990).

5   'L'Elixir de longue vie de l'empereur Guillaume', *Revue des tradi-
    tions populaires*, XII (1887), p. 569.

6 LONGEVITY IN A TIME OF IDEOLOGIES

1 There is an excellent chapter on Metchnikoff in Paul de Kruif, *Microbe Hunters* (New York, no date).

2 For a recent biography, see Jean Real, *Voronoff* (Paris, 2001).

3 Henri Guillemin, *Victor Hugo par lui-même* (Paris, 1951)

4 Hector Ghilini, *Le Secret du Dr Voronoff* (Paris, 1926).

5 For the communist project to transform the world, see my book *La Mythologie scientifique du communisme* (Paris, 2000), from which I have taken some of the examples and arguments set out here. On the 'new' Soviet biology, the most complete discussion is provided by Joël and Dan Kotek, *L'Affaire Lyssenko* (Brussels, 1986).

6 'The Jameson Satellite' was published in the July 1931 issue of the magazine *Amazing Stories*. The entire series can be found in Neil R. Jones, *The Planet of the Double Sun* (New York, 1967).

7 These words are cited by Gruman, *A History of Ideas about the Prolongation of Life*, p. 84.

8 Braunstein, 'Auguste Comte', p. 298.

7 THE RELIGION OF HEALTH

1 On this new 'religion', see Lucien Sfez, *La Santé parfaite: Critique d'une nouvelle utopie* (Paris, 1995) and *L'Utopie de la santé parfaite: Colloque de Cérisy*, ed. Lucien Sfez (Paris, 2001).

2 Immortality as a literary theme is the subject of Carl B. Yoke and Donald M. Hassler, eds, *Death and the Serpent: Immortality in Science Fiction and Fantasy* (Westport, CT, and London, 1985). In the following section I have chiefly drawn on the articles by Nick O'Dononhoe, 'Condemned to Life: "The Mortal Immortal" and "The Man Who Never Grew Young"', pp. 83–90; Joseph Sanders, 'Dancing on the Tightrope: Immortality in Roger Zelazny', pp. 135–43; Theodore Krulik, 'The Disease of Longevity: James Gunn's *The Immortals*', pp. 175–83; Gregory M. Shreve, 'The Jaded Eternals: Immortality and Imperfection in Jack Vance's *To Live Forever*', pp. 185–91.

3 Shreve, 'The Jaded Eternals', pp. 190–91.

4 Philippe Ariès, *Histoire des populations françaises et leurs attitudes*

devant la vie depuis le XVIIIe *siècle* (Paris, 1948, 2nd edn 1971);
L'Enfant et la vie familiale sous l'Ancien Régime (Paris, 1960, 3rd edn
1975).

5 This 'new youth' is analysed by Christian Lalive d'Epinay (in col-
laboration with Jean-François Bickel): 'La Retraite, voyage vers
Cythère ou rejet dans les limbes?', in *L'Imaginaire des âges de la vie*,
ed. Danièle Chauvin (Grenoble, 1996), pp. 281–303.

6 Philippe Ariès, *L'Homme devant la mort* (Paris, 1977); Norbert
Elias, *Über die Einsamkeit der Sterbenden in unseren Tagen*
(Frankfurt am Main, 1982).

7 Yves Christen, 'Longévité: Huit recettes pour ne pas vieillir', *Le
Figaro Magazine*, 26 December 1998, pp. 29–32. The recommended
recipes include 'French food and drink'.

8 'Les hommes en quête de look' (a study by Gérard Nirascou) in
Le Figaro, 28 November 1996, p. 12.

9 David Concar, 'Death of Old Age', *New Scientist*, 22 June 1996,
pp. 24–9; Jeffrey Kluger, 'Can We Stay Young?', *Time*, 9 December
1996, pp. 57–63. In this chapter I have made extensive use of
information taken from these two articles.

10 Roy Walford, *Maximum Life Span* (1983); Gabriel Simonoff,
La Nouvelle éternité: Bien vivre 120 ans (Paris, 1993).

11 Interview published in *Dimanche CH* [Lausanne], 29 April 2001,
p. 2.

12 *Le Moniteur du règne de la justice* [Paris], no. 18 (1995), p. 1.

13 On organ replacement (and other recent methods to obtain
longevity), see Michio Kaku, *Visions: How Science Will
Revolutionize the 21st Century* (1997).

14 A dossier on the subject of recent manifestations of longevity in
China was published by the newsletter *Ombres: Réalités parallèles*
(March–April 1995).

15 Claude Vorilhon, 'Raël', *Le Livre qui dit la vérité: Le Message donné
par les extra-terrestres* (Brantôme, 1974, 2nd edn 1977), pp. 143–5.

16 For an overview of this, see David Concar's article, 'Forever
Young', *New Scientist*, 22 September 2001, pp. 26–33.

Index